To my parents, without whom I wouldn't be here.

Acknowledgments

While my name may be on the cover, I can't take all the credit for the realization of this book. Without the support of my family and friends, the chance meetings with fantastic contacts along the course of my career, and the beast we call the Internet, this book would have never happened.

Special thanks to Kevin Wilkenson, the owner of SimplyMaya.com, who recommended me to Sybex. Working on this book meant that I couldn't produce any new tutorials for a few months; however, I hope many of you reading this will pay your own thanks by taking a look at the services www.SimplyMaya.com has to offer.

Great thanks to Steve Garcia who contributed the concept art for the satyr warrior. This book could have had any number of boring character designs, but Steve would have none of it! Quick congratulations to him for the birth of his first child, Caitlyn Joy Garcia.

Thanks to Arvee Garde for performing his martial arts mastery for the animation reference videos used in this book. For those interested, he trains in the Filipino martial art of Pekiti Tirsia Kali. He is also an instructor for the Texas Kali Association located in Austin. You can find more information about them at www.TexasKali.org.

Thank you as well to Michael Morlan for helping me with the filming. A great feature of this book wouldn't have been possible without his expertise and equipment. Check out his impressive body of work (and maybe hire him for some) at www.Michael-Morlan.net.

Big thanks to my co-workers: Eric P., John So., Steve, Michael Mo., Arvee, Tom, Ryan, John S., Dave, Wynne, Ben, Chip, John M., Sam, Jeff, Travis, Dan, Eric S., and Tommy! Thank you for putting up with me! Oh, and for that "job" thing, too.

And, of course, I have to thank everyone who withstood my bickering e-mails and finally conceded to contributing their profiles and art to this book. Steve Nelson, Jeff Hall, Mike Hovland, John Sommer, Danny Ngan, Jon Jones, Andrew Risch, Andrew Gerard, James Bradford, Grayson Chalmers, and Ben Mathis— Thank you!

I have to acknowledge the great people at Sybex and Alias who helped me take this journey of authorship. While I may have had the writing skills of a slow-witted primate, they quickly worked me into shape! Willem Knibbe, Mariann Barsolo, Rachel Gunn, Kathy Grider-Carlyle, and Keith Reicher, thank you very much! Maybe we can make another one soon.

And last, but certainly not least, thank you to my parents and family. As the dedication at the beginning says, without you, I wouldn't be here. And I don't just mean genetically. I love you all!

Philippians 4:13

Dear Reader

Thank you for choosing *The Game Artist's Guide to Maya*. This book is part of a new wave of Sybex graphics books, all written by outstanding authors—artists and teachers who really know their stuff and have a clear vision of the audience they're writing for. It's also part of our growing library of truly unique 3D animation books.

Founded in 1976, Sybex is the oldest independent computer book publisher. More than twenty-five years later, we're committed to producing a full line of consistently exceptional graphics books. With each title, we're working hard to set a new standard for the industry. From the paper we print on, to the writers and photographers we work with, our goal is to bring you the best graphics books available.

I hope you see all that is reflected in these pages. I'd be very interested to hear your comments and get your feedback on how we're doing. To let us know what you think about this, or any other Sybex book, please visit us at www.sybex.com. Once there, go to the product page, click on Submit a Review, and fill out the questionnaire. Your input is greatly appreciated.

Please also visit www.sybex.com to learn more about the rest of our graphics line.

Best regards,

DAN BRODNITZ
Associate Publisher—Graphics
Sybex Inc.

About the Author

Michael McKinley is an artist for Warthog Texas (www.warthogtx.com), a game developer in Austin, Texas. He also writes online learning material for Maya software, which can be found at www.SimplyMaya.com. Michael formerly helped teach Maya classes at Collins College in Tempe, AZ. More information about Michael and his projects can be discovered at his website: www.mtmckinley.net.

Contents

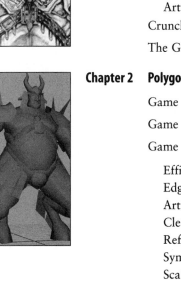

Chapter 6   Particle Effects   **193**

Introduction

Welcome to *The Game Artist's Guide to Maya*! Whether you're a current 3D Artist in the game industry or you're looking forward to becoming one, this book will help you learn the skills and techniques you need to become successful.

This is the first Maya Press title to focus on creating game art, and I hope you enjoy it!

What You Will Learn from This Book

The Game Artist's Guide to Maya will take you through the basic game art development pipeline, taking a concept from paper to reality. You'll also learn about the game industry as a whole and the different artist positions that are generally available. Profiles of current industry professionals are spread throughout the book. Top artisans discuss how Maya has been used in many top-selling games. Their insight into the field can help answer some of the questions aspiring game artists may have.

Who Should Read This Book

Anyone who is interested in working as an artist in the game industry, who has recently joined the field, or perhaps who is a veteran of the industry interested in new game art possibilities will find the contents of this book very useful. It goes over real-life responsibilities that game art professionals have to deal with on a daily basis.

How to Use This Book

The chapters in this book go through the normal development process that a piece of game art takes from start to finish. If you are just beginning with a brand new project, you should be able to get through the process in no time by going through each chapter sequentially. Also, you can use each chapter to help you through each step of the development process separately, as you find the need.

Before you begin, you'll need to have some basic Maya skills. For example, you should know how to navigate Maya's interface and how to use the Translate, Rotate, and Scale tools.

Discussed tools and commands are explained in detail, so even those coming from other applications should be able to recognize functions from what they're used to and apply them effectively.

How This Book Is Organized

Chapter 1: The Game Industry Before delving into art production, this first chapter gives you a quick introduction to how the game industry and the game development pipeline works. This chapter goes over the differences between Developers and Publishers and discusses the many different artist jobs that are out there. It also includes demo reel advice for when you're ready to get that game job!

Chapter 2: Polygonal Modeling Polygonal Modeling is the first step in creating art assets. This chapter shows you how to create a game model using a concept image as a guide and sticking to predetermined real-time modeling limitations, such as a polycount.

Chapter 3: Texturing This chapter demonstrates UV mapping and layout techniques that you can use when preparing a model for texturing. It also includes detailed information about texture formats, resolutions, and how to create the different kinds of textures games use (normal maps, specular maps, etc.).

Chapter 4: Rigging Before animation can take place, animation controls must be created through the process known as rigging. This chapter walks you through the process, from setting up a skeleton to preparing blend shapes, and more.

Chapter 5: Animation This chapter delves into the world of animating for games. It demonstrates techniques for creating animation clips that can blend between each other using the Trax Editor.

Chapter 6: Particle Effects Particle effects can be used to add that final pizzazz to a model's visual performance. This chapter goes over how to create such effects using sprites as well as animated geometry.

Artist Profiles Sidebars that profile current game art professionals from all over the country are spaced throughout the book. Their perspectives on the game industry, and how Maya is used in it, are sure to interest any aspiring game artist.

Maya in Games Sidebars talk about many hit games that were created using Maya. These discussions can help you recognize the types of game visuals you can achieve with the software.

Hardware and Software Considerations

Maya is quite the athlete these days, as the program is capable of running on many different operating systems and computer setups. Alias specifies what hardware and software are compatible with Maya at their website:

    http://www.alias.com/eng/support/maya/qualified_hardware/index.jhtml

In general terms, the faster the computer, the better. A nice, fast processor, a good chunk of RAM (memory), and a capable video card are all must-haves. A sizeable hard drive for storage is also very desirable. Here are some good numbers to shoot for:

- At least 2 to 2.5 GHz processor
- 512 MB to 1GB of RAM
- A good video card, such as the nVidia Quadro or ATI FireGL series
- 100GB or larger hard drive

The Book's CD

Concept Art: This folder contains high-quality concept images for the character that is created through the course of the book's instructions.

Images: This folder contains many sample high-resolution images of photo sources provided by the fine folks at www.3d.sk, one of the best human anatomy sources on the Internet. These images can be useful for anatomy reference or as texture sources. Also, any images needed for the tutorials can be found here.

Tutorials: This folder is divided into each chapter's specific section. Each chapter folder has the Maya project directories for the tutorials in question, which include saved stages of the character at almost every step of the way for easy reference.

Video: Divided into a couple sections, the Video folder has model stages and animation references. The model stages show videos of each major step in the tutorial's processes. The animation references contain many sample videos of martial arts moves you can use in Chapter 5, "Animation," and in your own projects.

Maya Personal Learning Edition 6

Also on the CD is the Maya Personal Learning Edition 6 (Maya PLE 6), the free version of Maya that gives you access to Maya Complete for noncommercial uses. With this free version, you can do everything in the tutorials. The software runs on Windows 2000/XP Professional and Mac OS.

Contact the Author

Michael can be contacted through his website at www.mtmckinley.net. He also frequents the message boards of www.SimplyMaya.com. Feel free to say hello or to ask any Maya questions you may have.

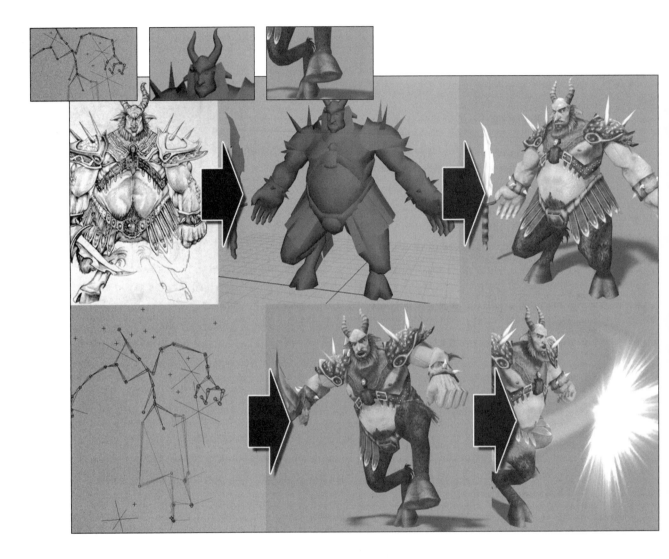

The Game Industry

For many aspiring digital artists, a job in the game industry is the dream of a lifetime. Whether it's fashioning fantastic worlds and characters from scratch or painstakingly re-creating accurate World War II submarines, the life of a game artist can be greatly rewarding. A game artist's career comes with its fair share of challenging times, however. The more you know early in your career, the better off you will be. Before you delve into learning the ins and outs of art production, take a moment to understand not only what is expected of you as a game artist, but also what the game industry is all about.

1

Chapter Contents
Developers and Publishers
Artist Jobs in the Industry
Demo Reels
The Game Development Pipeline

Developers and Publishers

More often than not, games are created through a partnership between two distinct companies known as a *developer* and a *publisher*. The developer is the company that actually creates the game—design, art, programming, etc. The publisher takes that game, markets it, and distributes it throughout the rest of the country or world.

The relationships between developers and publishers have evolved in many ways. These relationships are normally divided into three categories:

First-Party Developers

Second-Party Developers

Third-Party Developers

First-Party Developers These developers are entirely owned by their publishers. One example is Nintendo. In addition to being Nintendo, the creator of the Nintendo-brand gaming consoles (Game-Boy Advance, Nintendo Gamecube, and the Nintendo DS) and publisher of games, they are also Nintendo, the developer. Their trademark games, such as *Super Mario Brothers* and *The Legend of Zelda*, are games they create themselves using teams of developers under their employ.

Second-Party Developers These independent developers are not owned by a publisher. They have signed agreements giving a specific publisher the exclusive right to publish their titles. An example is Naughty Dog, the developer of popular titles such as *Crash Bandicoot* and *Jak & Daxter*. They have signed exclusive publishing rights to Sony.

 Note: The defining line between first-party and second-party developers is a thin one. Generally, a first-party developer can be considered an in-house department of the publisher, while a second-party developer is a separate entity.

Third-Party Developers These developers are the most common type. They sign contracts with a publisher on a per-game basis. In fact, many third-party developed games are released on multiple gaming platforms. Warthog is an example of this type of developer. They have developed games, such as *Harry Potter and the Philosopher's Stone*, for the Sony Playstation 2, Microsoft Xbox, and Nintendo Gamecube. For this particular title, Warthog partnered with Electronic Arts, a publisher that arranges distribution deals for all major game platforms.

Game Artist: Steve Nelson

Job Title Animator / 3D Artist

Studio Vicarious Visions

Credits *That's So Raven, Kids Next Door*

Studio Site www.vvisions.com

Personal Site www.stevenelsonanimator.com

Q. How and why did you get into the game industry?

A. I went to Savannah College of Art and Design, and graduated with a BFA in computer art with a focus in character animation. I have wanted to be an animator since the age of eight. I have wanted to play video games since the age of eight. There's only one way to do both and get paid for it.

Q. Describe your role at your studio.

A. Create animations and game assets for a variety of games and platforms.

Q. What has been the most inspirational to you in regard to your artwork?

A. I had a teacher in junior college that influenced me a lot, but to put it in terms that people can relate to I'd say Pixar (like every other computer animator), and the Loony Toons were huge. As well as the older Disney stuff like *Lady and the Tramp*.

Q. What is your favorite artistic style?

A. I'm a big fan of the cartoony art approach that games like *Beyond Good and Evil* and *The Legend of Zelda: The Windwaker* have taken. Although not to the point of it becoming Japanese Anime . . . just stylized.

Q. What is your favorite kind of game?

A. Oh, you're pressing me hard here. I'd say it's between real-time strategy, unique first-person shooters, and well-crafted role-playing games.

Q. How do you use Maya in your specific job?

A. Maya is used for everything from animation to level modeling. We use just about everything except things like cloth, fur, or high-detail rendering.

Q. What about Maya do you like better than other 3D applications?

A. The strongest animation toolset I have found in a 3D package to date.

Q. Which Maya tool could you not live without?

A. Definitely the Dope Sheet and Graph Editor (and the ability to manipulate within them directly).

Q. What advice might you have for the up-and-coming game artist?

A. Keep your nose against your computer screen. Spend more time learning your craft than anything else. As harsh as it sounds, the guy that puts forth the most effort usually comes out on top.

Artist Jobs

As an artist in the game industry, you will eventually work for a developer of some sort. But what jobs are available for someone of your talents? A variety of jobs are available in the art departments of game developers.

Note: The positions at game studios vary greatly. A 3D Artist at one studio may have a completely different set of responsibilities or duties compared to a 3D Artist at another. I can, however, give you a general idea of what you might expect in such positions. These generalizations should help you better understand the kinds of jobs available to you in this industry.

Junior Artist A Junior Artist is most likely the kind of job you can expect to find when first entering the industry. With little or no prior game experience, a Junior Artist will usually be hired into a company primarily to create background elements for the developing games and to learn about the development process.

Many studios hire Junior Artists on a temporary basis. These positions are used to ramp up the art staff to handle the stress period of the development schedule, eventually ramping back down as the game nears completion. You must prove that you are a capable and talented artist during these kinds of arrangements, so that you can increase your chances of becoming a permanent employee.

3D Artist The role of a 3D Artist (or Staff Artist) is fairly generic in title if not in duty. As unexciting as this position might sound, it could very well be the position with the most exciting variety of duties. As a 3D Artist, your duties could require you to create just about anything—vehicles and weapons, structures and environments, characters and creatures, planets and star fields, and beyond. In most cases, 3D Artists make up a large percentage of a studio's art department, and the position can be divided into three main categories:

> **Modeler** A Modeler is an artist responsible for creating the geometry, or shape, making up an object or character in a game. Modeling will be explained in greater detail in Chapter 2.

> **Texture Artist** A Texture Artist takes the completed 3D model and applies textures to create the "skin" of the object. In most cases, the same person acts as both the Modeler and the Texture Artist. The process of applying textures to a model will be explained in greater detail in Chapter 3.

> **Animator** An Animator is an artist who is responsible for rigging and animating the characters, creatures, etc., found in a game. They rarely are involved with the modeling or texturing of a game model. Instead, they focus on that model's movement. Rigging and animating a game model will be explained in greater detail in Chapters 4 and 5, respectively.

Concept Artist Concept Artists are responsible for creating the look of the game world. The Concept Artist uses traditional art mediums such as pencil and paper (or stylus and monitor) to illustrate ideas and concepts (environments, characters, vehicles, etc.). These designs, once approved, are then given to the 3D Artists to develop into the game.

Character Artist, Environment Artist, Etc. A Character Artist (or an Environment Artist) is a specialist who is responsible for creating (and sometimes animating) the characters and creatures or the environments and structures found in a game. Such specialized positions are generally filled at larger studios, where there are enough people to make such positions viable.

FX Artist An FX Artist (or Effects Artist) is responsible for creating the many particle effects found in games. These can range from weather effects like rain and snow to action effects like the flash of a gun barrel. The vast majority of such effects are done entirely with *sprites,* small planes that are affected by dynamic forces. Particle effects in games will be explained in greater detail in Chapter 6.

Technical Artist A Technical Artist is like a blend between an artist and a programmer. While they have the creative responsibilities of an artist, they also have the scripting and programming skills to create scripts and plug-ins for Maya or other applications to make the artists' jobs easier and more efficient.

A Technical Artist can also be responsible for creating setup tools, such as a common animation rig that is used for all of the characters in the game.

Cinematic Artist The art created for cinematics is generally done in much the same way that computer graphics are created in television and film, without the constraints or limitations of their in-game counterparts. If you want to be a Cinematic Artist, this book might not help you as much as it will help you with some of the other jobs in this list. For more information on this job position, see *Maya Character Animation, 2nd Edition,* by Jae-jin Choi (Sybex, 2004)

Senior Artist A Senior Artist is someone who more than likely has been in the industry for a number of years or who has a couple of published games on their résumé. They are generally the ones given more important responsibilities, such as main characters or other critical elements, in a game project.

Lead Artist Lead Artists are put in charge of a group of artists within a team. They ensure that their group follows instructions and accomplishes their goals on time. They are generally the first people who review a finished art asset before it is sent along on the approval process. While Lead Artists incorporate more management into their roles than most others, they also tend to have at least some art production duties of their own. Depending on the size of the team, a project can have any number of Lead Artists.

Art Director The Art Director holds the top position in the artist chain of command. His responsibilities focus on managing and scheduling the rest of the art staff, hiring and firing, and other such managerial duties.

Game Artist: Jeffrey T. Hall

Job Title Lead Game Design Instructor

Studio Formerly Acclaim Studios SLC, currently Collins College

Credits NBA Jam 2000, NBA Jam '99, Space Jam, VR Stalker, Return Fire, Secrets of the Luxor

Personal Site http://www.Flatheadgames.com/j_main.htm

Q. How and why did you get into the game industry?

A. I started out doing freelance 3D animation after taking some classes. I later began teaching the computer painting and computer animation courses as a student at BYU and did so for a while. My freelance partner/mentor/friend knew some people who were starting a game company, and we started working for them from day one.

Q. Describe your role at your studio.

A. My positions and duties varied from video editing to cameraman to cinematic lead to modeling to motion editing and, of course, animation. I have always seemed to be in mentor/training capacities when I worked in games, so when the opportunity to teach 3D Animation came my way, I took it.

Q. What is your favorite kind of game?

A. I tend to like shooters with RPG elements in them since I don't have the time to dedicate to games that I used to.

Q. How do you use Maya in your specific job?

A. I teach seven different classes in Maya, covering all the topics from modeling to MEL.

Q. What about Maya do you like better than other 3D applications?

A. I like Maya because it is a very robust tool that expects you to be an intelligent user, and is fairly user-friendly as well.

Q. Which Maya tool could you not live without?

A. For games, the Split Poly tool. In general, any of the spline surface creation tools.

Q. What advice might you have for the up-and-coming game artist?

A. Work very hard to know your craft inside and out. Be willing to spend lots of time staying up-to-date with the software and techniques for modeling efficient, effective props and characters.

Note: How much money does a game artist make? The answer is highly relative. The latest results (as of this writing) from the Game Development Salary Survey can be found at http://www.gamasutra.com/features/20040211/olsen_01.shtml.

It's becoming more and more common to find many of these positions combined into a single person's job. For example, most Modelers are also expected to be very capable Texture Artists. When browsing a studio's Help Wanted list, always keep the other job criteria in mind. Make sure that you are at least familiar with the whole process that goes into creating a piece of game art, as you never know when you may be called upon to pick up the slack in another department.

Getting the Job

Getting that foot in the door of a game development studio can be challenging. It's mostly a matter of the quality of your portfolio, but applying for the right job at the right time with a little bit of luck can be a big factor. If you don't have much luck in your first few attempts to find a job, have patience and keep trying. With a quality portfolio and the willingness to travel, you should eventually find a job.

Your portfolio is the most important tool you need to get that first job. I also recommend creating a website. Even something simple with only your portfolio of images and animation and an e-mail address is better than nothing. A website will give your potential employers something that is easy to click through, so they can get a good idea of your potential skill. Preparing a demo reel is definitely a good idea. Here are some demo reel tips:

Don't make your opening too long. An opening sequence that shows your name and contact info is fine, but don't make it too long. Two or three seconds should be enough. Don't forget that a viewer can pause it. Try to make sure any blank, silent time before the reel starts is as short as possible. Employers can be pretty impatient, and if they don't see something within a few seconds, they might just discard the reel before it starts.

Put your best work first. Many employers might not have the patience to view an entire reel, or they may simply not have the time. Putting your best work up front will get their interest early, which may entice them to watch the rest of the demo. If a weak piece is the first thing they see, they may not wait to see the awesome work you display later.

Use a pleasant music track. A reel doesn't necessarily need to be an audio extravaganza, but you should put some sort of music to your reel to keep the viewer's ears busy. Silence during a reel's playback can seem boring, even if the work being shown is good. Adding that little aural touch can help make watching your reel a more appealing experience, which is always a good thing!

Keep it short and sweet. Try to limit the length of your reel to two or three minutes. As it approaches the four-minute mark, no matter how good the work is, employers may start looking at their watches. Get their attention with a short, high-quality reel. If you have additional work, they can look at your website or request more directly from you.

Don't dwell too long on a single piece. When your reel is short, focusing on a single piece for thirty seconds or more may seem conspicuously like padding your reel for length. Don't be afraid to have a shorter reel, but make sure the work is your best.

Keep your reel focused. Customize your reel for the job to which you are applying. If you are applying for a Modeler/Texture Artist position, don't have too much animation or other, off-topic work. Otherwise, you're just wasting the employer's time. If applying to different kinds of jobs, make multiple reels that focus on the jobs in question.

Label your work accurately. Make sure that the employer understands what your contribution is to the work they are viewing. If you collaborated with a group to complete a certain piece of work, send a *breakdown sheet*, a description of the reel that details the project title, what the piece was used for, and your role in its creation. This way employers can focus on your work and not someone else's. If you did all the work yourself, say so.

Be kind. Rewind. Possibly the most frequently committed mistake that job candidates make is forgetting to rewind their reels before sending them to potential employers. Don't forget to rewind your VHS reel before you submit it.

Note: Make sure you carefully read the submission requirements of a job ad. Many will specifically ask for a website or a VHS reel rather than other, more-modern media. CDs and DVDs are not as desirable because of the many different DVD brands and audio/video codecs out there that potentially won't work on their players. In contrast, a VHS tape works with any VCR.

Art Tests

Employers frequently ask applicants to complete an art test. This is usually a good sign, because it means they are interested in you for the job and they want to see how you perform a given task.

Art tests are also given to make sure that the work you are taking credit for is actually yours. If you deliver an out-of-this-world demo reel, but your art test results are poor, they may call into question your truthfulness.

But in most cases, the art test is to gauge your performance for their current project. After all, you may have shown in your demo reel that you can create awesome skyscrapers and motor bikes, but can you do just as well with a war elephant and a halfling tree camp? The art test will find out. Make sure you're prepared.

Crunch Time

The thought of creating games is obviously very appealing. One common misconception, however, is that working at a game studio means you're just playing games all day. That could not be further from the truth! In fact, your game-playing time might dwindle because of the amount of work that is involved. It *can* be fun work, but it *is* work just the same.

Most people interested in game development have heard of the dreaded *crunch time*. This refers to a period of time in a game's development schedule where overtime is mandatory in order to meet fast-approaching deadlines. What was once a fairly mild 9-hour day, suddenly balloons to 12, 15, or more hours a day. Crunch time can potentially last weeks or even months on end.

The best way to avoid massive amounts of crunch time is to do your best to get things done efficiently, accurately, and on schedule during your normal workday. Some crunch should probably be expected. However, if everyone on a project works together and makes full use of their time, it can be minimized.

The Game Development Pipeline

The art production pipeline is the path that a game object takes from beginning to end, from conception to effects. This path actually comprises only one facet of the overall Game Development Pipeline. Understanding the pipeline processes early is a great asset to potential employers, as it gets you that much closer to being able to contribute to it. The average development pipeline is as follows:

1. **Design**

   Writers and Designers are critical parts of any game's development. They are the ones who actively birth the idea that eventually becomes a game you see on the shelf. They come up with the story and the overall gameplay mechanic. These ideas are then passed on to the Concept Artist.

2. **Conception**

   Concept Artists receive the documents that describe the game's characters and world. They visually interpret the ideas, creating dozens of sketches and paintings before they finally finding that perfect look for the game. This is an important step in the development of a piece of game art. When a character concept has been completed and approved, it moves on to the Modeler.

3. **Modeling**

   A Modeler takes the approved character concept art and uses that information to create a 3D model that can ultimately be used in the game. However, it must first go to texturing.

4. **Texturing**

   Once modeled, the 3D object must be textured. Textures are primarily created with a 2D program like Adobe Photoshop. After textures are applied, the character model continues on to be rigged.

5. **Rigging**

   Rigging can be done either by a specialized Technical Artist or by the Animator herself. Rigging, as described in Chapter 4, is the creation of animation controls that can be manipulated to create movement. Once the controls are in place, the character can travel to the Animator.

6. **Animation**

   With the animation controls in place, animation can commence. The Animators will perform any number of actions with the character model, as if they were manipulating a marionette—a highly complex, digital marionette, but a puppet just the same. When the finished model's performance actions are approved, the model can then go to the FX Artist.

7. **Special FX**

   All that is left in the art production part of this pipeline is adding the eye candy effects. The FX Artists can use any number of tools to jazz things up. They usually use custom tools developed for the game in question. Once the character's journey through the art pipeline has completed, it's exported to the programmers.

8. **Programming**

   While the artists were hard at work creating this character, the programmers were hammering away at their own workstations. They created code for the express purpose of giving our completed character a personality. Before it is used, however, the model must make one more trip. This time to the Level Designers.

9. **Level Design**

Using custom tools, the Level Designers place the newly completed character into a level in the game, ready to meet the players who later will purchase the finished product.

Thus ends the life cycle of an art asset. Make way for the next one. Now that you understand how games and game assets are made, let's get started on one of your own.

Maya in Games: Halo

Genre First-Person Shooter

Developer Bungie

Publisher Microsoft

Platform Xbox

Halo is the epitome of the great First-Person Shooter (FPS), and is arguably considered *the* best FPS ever made. You play the venerable Master Chief, fighting against the evils that make up the alien Covenant. In doing so, you make use of multiple weapons and vehicles throughout the game as you traverse the mysterious elliptical ring-world known as Halo.

As a flagship title for Microsoft's XBox, *Halo* showed exactly what the system was capable of. Giving players great graphics, great atmosphere, and great game play, it quickly became a top seller. Look for *Halo 2* to give players even better graphics, a better atmosphere, and better game play.

Courtesy of Microsoft Corporation © 2004. Microsoft, Halo, and Xbox are trademarks or registered trademarks of Microsoft Corp.

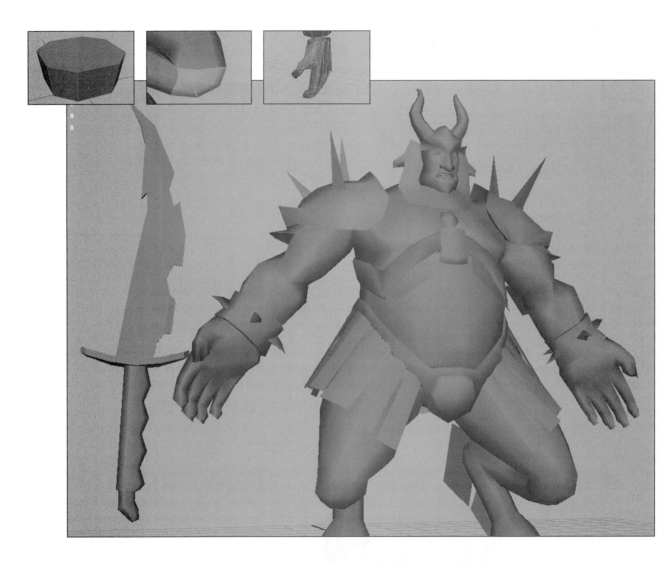

Polygonal Modeling

Polygons are the backbone of all game art. Practically everything you see on the screen is composed of them. As technology increases and consoles and computers are able to handle more and more polygons, the sheer number of objects on the screen and their overall complexity can increase in tandem. But even with the highest polygon thresholds, artists must still perform within some form of boundary. In this chapter, you will be introduced to the basic tools used in the construction of polygonal models, and you will also be introduced to important methods, concepts, and working practices that you can utilize in any game project.

Chapter Contents

Game Art Limitations

As you probably already know, *polygons* (or *polys*) are geometric figures that make up the vast majority of all game art. They are constructed using a series of coordinates in 3D space that project a surface between them. The main components of a polygon are listed here:

Vertex. A vertex is a single point in *XYZ space* (XYZ being a representation of width, height, and depth). At least three vertices must be present to create a polygon.

Edge. An edge is the direct line between two vertices.

Face. A face is the projected surface between three or more vertices.

UV. These components are single points that represent coordinates on a texture. We will discuss UVs in much greater detail in the next chapter.

These different components are accessible by right-clicking on a model and selecting the component type in the marking menu that appears. You can also access these components by clicking the Select by Component Type button in the Status line and choosing the desired element from the available selection masks.

One of the first things you'll need to come to terms with in the field of game art is polygon limitations. No matter what game you work on, no matter how powerful the system, you will always have some sort of limit that restricts you. In the case of games, this is generally referred to as the *polycount,* or the number of polygons of which a single model is composed. In all cases, the number you are counting refers to *triangle polygons* (or *tris*). If you create a polygon that has four sides (a *face* or *quad*), it is counted as two triangle polygons.

In order to help you keep track of your polygon usage, Maya has a polygon counter. You can find it under **Display > Heads Up Display > Polycount.** While the counter is active, you will have a heads-up display (HUD) of the polygon usage in the upper-left corner of all your view ports (Figure 2.1).

Polycounts can vary heavily from game to game; therefore, successful game artists need to be able to create quality art using all sorts of polycounts. Your art director will let you know what kind of polycounts are used in your project. Some of the criteria used to determine polycounts include:

Number of Characters/Objects on the Screen at the Same Time In a real-time strategy (RTS) game such as *Conquest* or *Warcraft*, you deal with multiple players. Each player controls armies of various sizes that fight each other on a single playing field. A lot of soldiers, tanks, spaceships, monsters, and other kinds of units can potentially be interacting on the screen at one time. In order for the game to be playable, each of the units must be composed of a fairly low number of polygons. The number of polygons is determined by their overall size compared to the average unit and by the overall capability of the game engine with which you are working. A single unit could be as low as 50 to 100 polygons. In a fighting game like *Mortal Kombat* or *Soul Caliber*, on the other hand, where you have at maximum two characters on the screen at any given time, your polygon limit can be quite high (for example, 4000 to 5000 or more).

Prominence on the Screen Some games may not have hundreds of units on the screen, but most do have at least one central figure, known as a *hero character*, that attacks and interacts with the player or other objects and creatures in the game. The hero can be very prominently displayed on the screen, and some games even allow you to zoom right into the character's face. In order to give such a figure aesthetic appeal, and to keep it believable, more polygons are used to give the hero more detail and lessen the jagged polygon look. Conversely, the hundreds of nameless secondary characters are never given that much screen time, and they are usually dispatched before the player really notices them. So, these models' polycounts could be significantly lower.

Type of Game Some game types may limit the polycounts of some models because of the type of game it is. A Massively Multiplayer Online Game (MMOG), for example, has hundreds if not thousands of players connecting to a server and playing together. One way to help speed the transfer of information from server to player and back again is to limit file sizes. A lower polycount, as well as smaller texture files, might help in this regard.

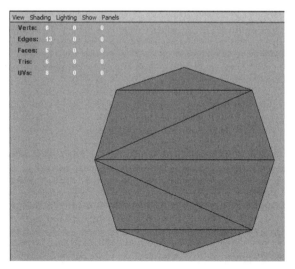

Figure 2.1 The polycount HUD shows you how many faces and tris are in your scene.

Game Modeling Common Tools and Commands

Keep in mind that people use many different modeling methods and techniques. All of the techniques are effective and have their pros and cons. It really comes down to the artist and his or her personal preference.

What I generally tend to do, and what I believe is the most common method, is use the default polygon primitives (found under **Create > Polygon Primitives**). Using the polygon editing tools described in the following text, I manipulate these shapes into the desired model. For characters, I recommend forming basic body parts separately—a cylinder becomes an arm, a sphere becomes the head, etc. Once these parts have been formed, they can be merged into the rest of the body to form the whole.

As with any art form, practice makes perfect. Study anatomy and even study other games very closely. The next time you run Frodo through an evil Mordor castle, take a moment and examine your character's construction. Look around the environment and train your eye to notice how the models are actually put together.

For our project in this book, we will go for a polycount of between 3000 to 3500 triangle polygons. This is a good medium range for a hero model that could potentially fit in most game types. First, we'll go over some of the more common tools and commands that are involved in polygonal modeling for games. When other, less common tools are used, I will go over them within the tutorial.

Create Polygon Tool (**Polygons** > Create Polygon Tool in the Modeling Module) The Create Polygon tool (Figure 2.2) allows you to create a custom polygonal shape. This is useful for situations where the polygon primitives that are provided by Maya might not serve as a good starting point for the object you have in mind. Once the tool is active, simply placing points one at a time will create a preview of the polygonal shape you are making. When the desired shape has been formed, simply press Enter to finish the creation, and make the shape into a valid polygon. From this point, you can manipulate it further to create whatever your heart desires.

Because this tool requires point placement by the user, I recommend using one of the orthographic views (Front, Side, or Top). This way, you can control the tool with pinpoint accuracy.

Append to Polygon Tool (**Polygons** > Append to Polygon Tool in the Modeling Module) The Append to Polygon tool's primary purpose is to fill holes and patch deleted faces (Figure 2.3). While the tool is active, the border edges of your model will highlight a thicker green. Once your first border edge is selected, you will usually see purple arrows pointing in the surface's optimal surface direction. Following the arrows' indicated directions, continue to click on the bordering edges until the hole is filled. Press the Enter key to finalize your action.

Figure 2.2 Use the Create Polygon tool to create custom shapes easily.

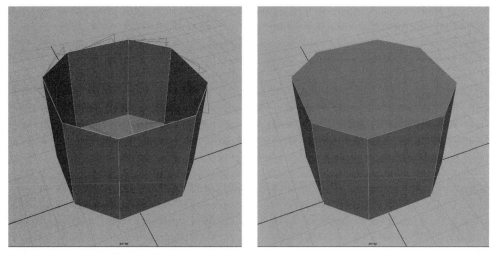

Figure 2.3 The Append to Polygon tool is very useful for filling gaps and holes.

The Append to Polygon tool can also be used to add faces to an object using point placement. When using the tool in this manner, I recommend using the orthographic view ports for the most accuracy.

Split Polygon Tool (Edit Polygons > Split Polygon Tool in the Modeling Module) This is probably the most useful tool you will find in your polygonal editing arsenal. You can use the Split Polygon tool (Figure 2.4) to cut into your models to add detail, fix edge flow, and continue to create your model efficiently. Here are a few guidelines you should remember when you use the Split Polygon tool:

- Always start on an edge. You cannot begin a cut in the middle of a face.
- You cannot cut "through" an edge. You must click from edge to edge in order to continue your cut, and you cannot jump an edge in the process.

- Always end on an edge. As with starting the cut, it must end on an edge and not in the middle of a face.
- Press the Enter key to finalize your action.

Extrude Face and Extrude Edge (Edit Polygons > Extrude Face or Extrude Edge in the Modeling Module) This is another extremely useful and often-used coupling of tools. The Extrude Face and Extrude Edge commands (Figure 2.5) allow you to grab the chosen component and, just like the tool sounds, extend that component out from its original location, creating new geometry in between.

Figure 2.4 The Split Polygon tool can be used to add fine detail to an object.

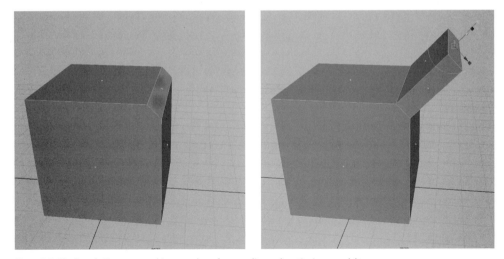

Figure 2.5 The Extrude Face command is a must-have for extending and continuing a model.

The gizmo that it uses can be confusing at first. However, it is essentially the Rotate, Translate, and Scale tools all combined into one. Use the arrowheads to translate, the small boxes to scale, and the circles to rotate. One thing to keep in mind is that some aspects of the tool become available only when you actively click to use a certain part of it. For example, by default, the only rotate handle that is visible is aligned to the camera. In order to bring up the X, Y, and Z rotation handles, simply click on the aligned handle and they will appear. Similarly, when you click one of the X, Y, or Z scale handles, the blue Scale All handle becomes available.

Merge Vertices (Edit Polygons > Merge Vertices in the Modeling Module) Although there are a couple of different merging commands, the one I consistently use in all of my projects is Merge Vertices (Figure 2.6). When you try to use this command on a selected number of points, nothing may appear to happen because of the tool's default options. Open the Merge Vertices option box and adjust the Distance slider. The larger the distance, the farther apart two or more vertices can be and still merge together.

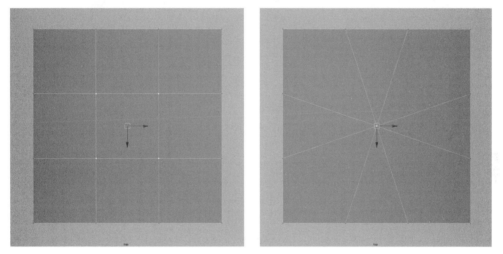

Figure 2.6 Merging vertices to remove geometry

Snapping Commands Snapping one component or object to another can be enormously helpful in creating some shapes and objects. The shortcut commands for the three main snapping options are listed here:

- X for Snap to Grids (or Grid Snap)
- C for Snap to Curves (or Curve Snap)
- V for Snap to Points (or Point Snap)

Note: You can also use the toggle buttons in the Status line to turn snapping on and off.

Bevel (**Edit Polygons** > Bevel in the Modeling Module) Bevel (Figure 2.7) is a function that chamfers the selected edge(s) or the surrounding edges of a selected face. You will usually need to adjust the options in the Channel Box after you perform the command to tweak it to the desired result.

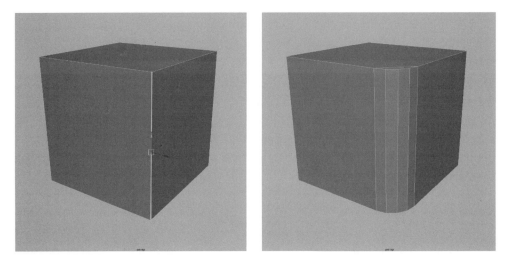

Figure 2.7 The result of a Bevel command

Triangulate and Quadrangulate (**Polygons** > Triangulate or Quadrangulate in the Modeling Module) Unlike some 3D applications, Maya does not automatically triangulate your meshes. Having triangle faces will ensure that your geometry is *planar* (flat) so your model will display correctly in the game. While the game engine will usually triangulate a model upon export, previewing the results in Maya can be beneficial. Using the Triangulate command (Figure 2.8), it will convert your geometry into three-sided faces. The Quadrangulate command will attempt to convert your geometry into four-sided faces as well. This tool does not necessarily work perfectly every time, so undoing the Triangulation is usually preferred.

Flip Triangle Edge (**Edit Polygons** > Flip Triangle Edge in the Modeling Module) In the case of modeling for games, this tool is a life saver. Game models are almost always triangulated when they are in the actual game to ensure planarity, whether or not the model itself is. So, essentially, the game engine triangulates the model for you. Sometimes, the method by which it does this may be unsatisfactory, or even incorrect. The following pictures demonstrate just how drastic a simple flip of an edge can change a model.

To use the command, select the edge in question and activate Flip Triangle Edge (Figure 2.9) from the menu. This command will not work in a few situations. First of all, the edge has to border two triangle faces. Secondly, if the edge in question is a UV border, it cannot flip. (We'll talk about UVs in the next chapter.)

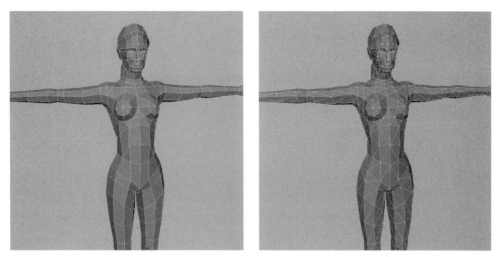

Figure 2.8 The result of a Triangulate command

Collapse (Edit Polygons > Collapse) The Collapse command is extremely useful for removing unneeded geometry. To use it, select an edge or face and choose the command from the menu. The selected components will collapse on themselves, effectively removing them from the model.

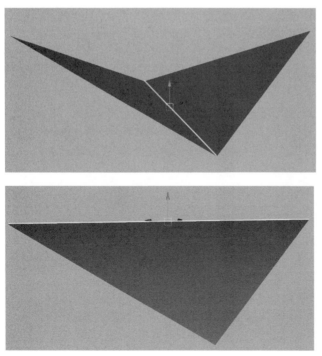

Figure 2.9 An example of how drastically a single flipped edge can change a model

Game Artist: Mike Hovland

Job Title Technical Artist

Studio Midway Games

Credits NBA Ballers, Cyberstrike 2

Studio Site www.midway.com

Q. How and why did you get into the game industry?

A. I started my career at a small Television/Film production studio in Chicago. When the studio had to make a choice between buying an Avid editing system or paying my wage, the Avid won out. The next job I was able to get was in games at a small startup studio in Virginia, and I haven't been able to get out of games since.

Q. Describe your role at your studio.

A. I am involved on a daily basis in art creation for the games, as well as technical aspects of the art creation—problem solving, pipeline issues, and tool writing inside of Maya to help minimize the drudgery of art creation.

Q. What has been the most inspirational to you in regard to your artwork?

A. Here at Midway, we have a large number of people who are incredibly talented and who have been in the industry for many years. I work side by side with some of the original creators of the games I grew up playing in the arcades. I draw my inspiration from all the talent around me at work. Some of these guys know more about creating games than I am likely to ever learn. It is incredibly rewarding being able to talk to the people who invented the games that launched so many other people into the game business.

Q. What is your favorite artistic style?

A. I prefer fantasy style art. I don't mean swords and sorcery per se, but I tend to lean toward the styles of artwork that aren't based on reality. I personally feel that not being confined to "does it look real?" to be much more rewarding.

Q. What is your favorite kind of game?

A. I tend to gravitate to the first-person shooters and any of the twitch styles of gaming.

Q. How do you use Maya in your specific job?

A. Maya is used for all the art creation in the games. If it is 3D and in the game, it came out of Maya. We use Maya for the environments and the characters. I write all my tools and exporters in Maya Embedded Language (MEL).

Continues

Game Artist: Mike Hovland *(Continued)*

Q. What about Maya do you like better than other 3D apps?

A. Maya's customizability is huge. The ability to set up Maya to fit your personal work style is a great thing.

Maya's scriptability is another aspect that I think is amazing, and one of the most powerful features of the software. I haven't come up against any problem that I couldn't solve through scripting yet. I've had many things that would probably be better off implemented as a plug-in, strictly for speed reasons, but MEL provides access to everything I have needed to write so far. Of course now someone reading this will see it as a challenge, and they will send me something that I can't implement with MEL, but I'm up for the challenge.

MEL also provides a means to prototype potential tools that could be implemented as a plug-in. You can write MEL code to test more advanced tools, as proof of concept that you can then show to programmers to implement as plug-ins for the software.

Q. Which Maya tool could you not live without?

A. MEL, MEL, and MEL.

Q. What advice might you have for the up-and-coming game artist?

A. Don't underestimate the importance of having traditional skills. It is much easier to illustrate a point using pencil and paper than to build it in 3D. I'm not suggesting that you have to be an accomplished fine artist, but you should be able to throw together a quick sketch to get your ideas across.

Don't overestimate the importance of software knowledge. I have found that if someone's demo reel shows that they have the basic skills for 3D work, I can teach them the software we use. Concentrate on developing the core skills necessary to successful game art creation.

Game Modeling Pointers

Before we start our project, you'll want to learn and perfect a few game modeling practices:

- Efficiency
- Edge flow (or geometry flow)
- Articulation
- Cleanup
- Reference usage
- Symmetry
- Scale and orientation

These will come easier with practice, and they will help you enormously as you begin your game art career. I will touch on them now and again throughout the tutorial, but you will definitely want to keep them in mind as you go about any project.

Efficiency

Even if given a high polycount, you should always strive for efficient modeling. Make sure that every polygon in a model is there for a real reason and not there just to meet a quota. Does that polygon add detail, definition, or articulation to the model? Does it serve any real purpose? If not, delete it or put it someplace where it will. Do not feel that polycounts must be met. If you have a 2000 poly limit and you finish a model with 30 to spare, look for places to use them. However, don't feel as if you failed by not meeting a certain number.

Here's another rule of thumb: Don't start out with too much geometry. Add geometry as you need it. Working this way is easier, and it will help you keep under your polycounts.

Edge Flow

As much as possible, keep the edges flowing along the surface in a way that follows the contours of the shape. This will result in a more natural, clean look. Doing so will also help keep your creation efficient and deformable for animation. When you are creating characters and creatures, use anatomy as your guide. Have the edges of the arm flow along the major muscle groups to make them seem that much more life like (Figure 2.10).

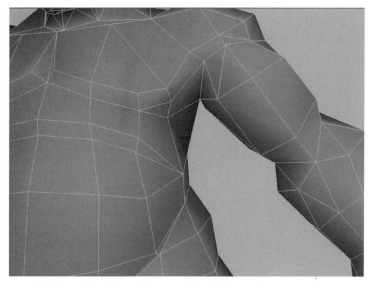

Figure 2.10 A good edge flow can help your model animate properly.

Articulation

When animating, you must have enough geometry in place at the joints for good *articulation* (or movement). You can use several methods to allow clean deformation to create movement. The one we will talk about in this book uses a V-joint technique (Figure 2.11). By orienting the edges of most joints in a V formation, you can almost always achieve good articulation.

Figure 2.11 An example of a V-joint

Articulating the face is a bit different than articulating a model's bendable joints. Facial articulation can rely mostly on edge flow and the amount of geometry budgeted to improve the face's range of expression.

Cleanup

Although you do want to use the previously mentioned methods while you are creating the model, some form of cleanup usually needs to happen toward the end of the process. The cleanup process consists of making changes to a model to help make it more efficient, make it have better edge flow, improve its articulation, or (most important) maintain its required polycount.

The most common cleanup work involves keeping a model within your given polycount. No matter how judicious you are during the creation process, you probably won't hit your mark on the first pass. Even if you do, you may want to tweak your creation and move some polygons away from one area and add them to another. For instance, at the end of the modeling phase you might decide that your character's face needs help with articulation. You could clean up other areas to gain the polys you need for your character's face. Subtracting from less critical areas to add polys to a more critical area will help keep the poly usage efficient and under your required polycount.

Reference Usage

I cannot stress enough the importance of good references. In nearly every project that I have been involved in or have witnessed, the ones that have good reference images (whether they be hand-drawn or photographs) have always been of higher quality then those without. The Internet is your one-stop shop for practically anything you could ever want in regard to photographs, blueprints, and schematics. I also highly recommend a digital camera for taking your own photographs to use as reference or texture sources. A mirror can really help you see how your own body and face move. You can use yourself as a model to achieve more realism in your work.

⊙ You will find a number of reference types, including concept art for the character modeling, photo sources for textures, and video for animation, on this book's CD.

Symmetry

Using symmetry can help cut down the amount of time it takes to complete a project. You can create half of the model and mirror a duplicate for the other side. Afterward, you can go back and add small details to avoid complete symmetry.

With that in mind, creating your models centered on the axis lines of the grid is a good idea. This way, you can use the grid easily for accurate mirroring.

Scale and Orientation

When you are involved with a major game project, scale and orientation are important factors to nail down early in the project's development. To streamline the process of getting your models from Maya to the game, make everything match according to its scale and orientation. This will save you a lot of headaches when it comes time to actually use your work in the game. If your car is the size of a skyscraper and your space station can fit in the palm of your main character's hand, fixing them and getting things proportioned can be time consuming. Spending a little time with a common scale and orientation setup can save you valuable minutes at crunch time.

 Note: Worrying about scale and orientation is not necessarily as important to our project in this book because it is a single character. However, in a real-life development situation, it can be quite critical.

Exporting

Someday you may need to export your completed model from one application to another. Your project's chosen animation application could be something other than Maya, for example. In such situations, it is common to export the model as an OBJ file.

To activate that option, make sure that `objExport.mll` has been turned on under **Window** > **Settings/Preferences** > **Plug-In Manager**. With this plug-in active, the OBJ option is available when you use **File** > **Export All or Selection**.

Not all applications are able to read OBJ file formats by default, so you may need to have your OBJ file converted into a different file format to use in your chosen application. One program called "Deep Exploration" is very useful for this, as it has the options available for converting your OBJ file into a variety of other formats for other applications.

Tutorial: Creating the Weapon

It is time to get started on our project. First, let us take a look at the character we will be creating. On the book's CD, open the `ConceptArt` directory. Here, you will find two images: `satyr_front.tif` and `satyr_side.tif`. These are the front and side views for our Satyr Warrior character Silenus, who legend says was the oldest satyr and served as a teacher to the mythical Dionysus. Silenus is quite an imposing figure, but even he would not last long in battle without his mighty sword. To ease into the modeling process, we will make sure he is well armed before we tackle the character himself.

In addition to the character drawings, the CD in the back of this book contains all the images, movies, and files that you need to work through the tutorials in this book. You will also find fantastic photo sources for textures and files for the interim stages of the tutorials.

Creating the Blade

To create the Blade, simply follow along with these steps.

1. Go to `Tutorials/Chapter2` and copy the directory named `Project_Sword` to your hard drive. Open the `Sword_Start.mb` file within the Scenes folder of this directory. To help you begin creating it, this scene contains an image plane of the sword by itself.

   If Maya can't find the image, you may need to set your project. Go to **File** > **Project** > **Set** and select the `Project_Sword` directory and click OK.

2. Enter Smooth Shade All or Flat Shade All from the front view's Shading menu (or press the 5 key). Also, turn on Hardware Texturing (or press the 6 key) to make the image visible within your view. While still in the front view, use the Create Polygon tool to create a polygon that follows the shape of the blade pictured (Figure 2.12).

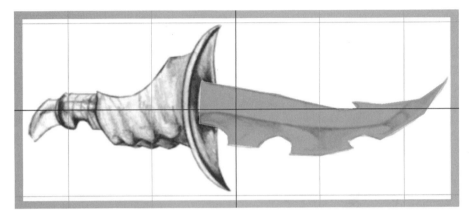

Figure 2.12 Use the Create Polygon tool to begin the blade.

Feel free to use your imagination to create your own unique weapon for your project. For now, do not concern yourself with polycounts too much. However, remember that we *are* making a game model here, so try to be judicious.

Note: Seeing your reference image behind your shaded geometry can be helpful. One way to accomplish this is to apply a new material to your geometry and raise the material's transparency in the Attribute Editor. You will then be able to see the image through your shaded geometry.

3. Using the Split Polygon tool, cut along the length of the blade along the indicated area on the drawing (Figure 2.13). This point of the surface will mark where the blade begins to taper to a sharpened edge.

4. Select **Polygons > Triangulate** to triangulate the model.

5. With the model still selected, extrude the faces out (**Polygons > Extrude Face**) approximately 0.057 units, giving the sword its initial thickness. This will extrude the faces of the entire model at once. Selecting the individual faces can have varying results.

Make sure the Keep Faces Together option is turned on. You can find it under **Polygons > Tool Options.**

6. Select the edges along the edge of the blade that will be sharp, and go to **Edit Polygons > Collapse** (Figure 2.14).

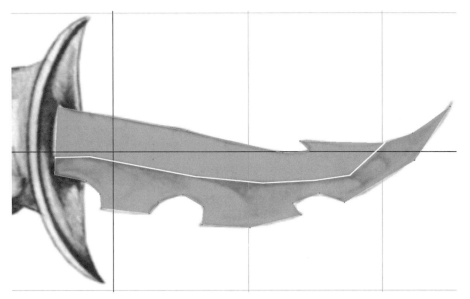

Figure 2.13 Split the shape along the blade.

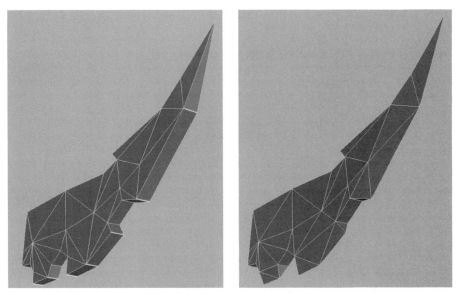

Figure 2.14 Use the Collapse command on the edges to make the blade appear sharp.

7. Before we create the hilt, select the faces that the hilt will cover on the end of the blade and delete them. When geometry is covered and won't be seen, you might as well remove it.

Note: Using the sword.tif drawing as your modeling guide is very important and useful. If I do not mention an exact length or number when we perform certain commands, use the drawing as a guide. This is easiest using the orthographic views such as the front and side view.

Creating the Hilt and Grip

To create the hilt and grip, just follow these steps.

1. For the curved hilt, create a polygon cube (**Create > Polygon Primitives > Cube**). Position it at the end of the blade object, and scale it to the approximate thickness you want to use for the hilt (around .07 units wide). In the Channel Box, you should see the polyCube1 creation options under the Inputs section. Here, we will adjust the number of divisions along the height of the cube to 4. Scale the rows of vertices about 50 percent to taper the tips (Figure 2.15).

2. The sword in the drawing is a bit pointed. Use the Split Polygon tool to add an edge to the top and bottom of the hilt and pull them out. Next, move the rows of vertices forward, toward the blade, to curve the hilt, as you see in Figure 2.16.

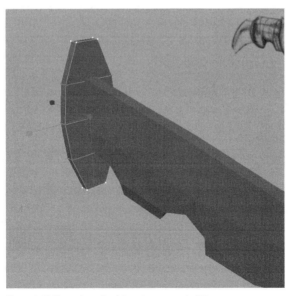

Figure 2.15 Taper the ends of the cube to start the hilt.

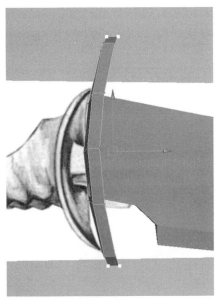

Figure 2.16 Curve the hilt.

3. For the sword's grip, we will create a polygon primitive cylinder. Position and scale the cylinder at the hilt, adjusting the creation options in the Channel Box under Inputs. Use these settings:

- Subdivisions Axis: 8
- Subdivisions Height: 8
- Subdivisions Caps: 0

4. For every other row of faces, select the three faces on the bottom. Using the Extrude Face command, extrude these faces down about .05 units and scale them about 50 percent to start creating the details of the grip (Figure 2.17).

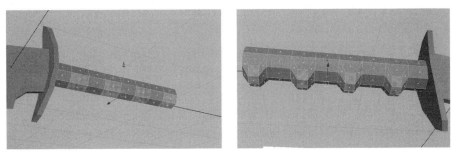

Figure 2.17 Extrude these faces down.

5. Now select the horizontal edges of these faces, and use the Collapse command to remove the unneeded geometry. Next, select the upper edge of these pointed edges and again use the Collapse command (Figure 2.18). Shorten or lengthen the handle to the desired size. After the character is finished, you can always change this to fit the sword to the hand.

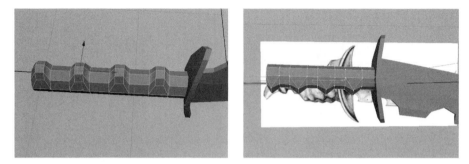

Figure 2.18 Remove unneeded geometry.

6. For the tooth-like knob on the end of the sword's grip, select the face on the end and extrude it out a couple times, scaling the extruded faces and positioning them to match the drawing (Figure 2.19).

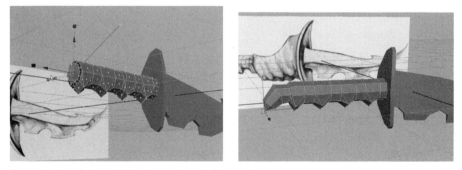

Figure 2.19 Extrude the tooth-like object on the end of the sword's grip.

At this point, the sword's overall shape is pretty much done. Let's go back and perform some cleanup.

7. Remove any faces that are not visible. Many of the faces currently on the sword grip can be removed using the Collapse command on their selected edges. After a bit of cleanup, we end up with something similar to Figure 2.20.

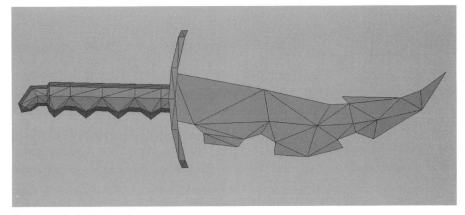

Figure 2.20 The finished sword

Tutorial: Creating the Character Model

Now, that we have a weapon for him, let's start on Silenus the Satyr Warrior. Many thanks to Steve Garcia for the fantastic concept art! This character should definitely get an aspiring game artist's feet wet in exactly the kinds of character projects to expect in the gaming industry.

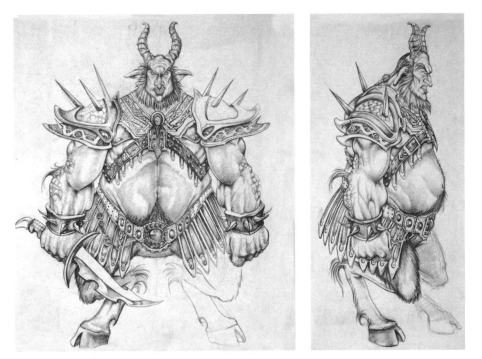

Concept art by Steve Garcia.

Maya in Games: Sly Cooper

Genre Stealth Adventure

Developer Sucker Punch Productions

Publisher Sony

Platform PlayStation 2

The *Sly Cooper* games (*Sly Cooper and the Thievius Raccoonus* and *Sly Cooper 2: Band of Thieves*) follow the exploits of Sly, a raccoon thief as he jumps, slides, and steals his way through expertly-designed, cartoon-shaded worlds. Aside from looking gorgeous, the game play is top-notch with fluid animation and easy-to-learn/hard-to-master controls. In fact, the only real complaint (if you can call it that) that almost everyone agrees on is that it's too short! Thankfully, the sequel should alleviate that problem.

The animation in these games is definitely worth sitting up and taking notice. Each character moves in ways that characterize the animal that they are based on. For example, Murray the hippo waddles comically while bashing enemies with his fists, and Bentley the turtle moves a little slower while using his invented weapons for ranged attacks. The cartoon-shaded worlds are truly fun to run around in, as it really seems like you're playing in a real cartoon. If you're keen on creating your own cartoony game characters, you'll want to check this one out. Definitely recommended.

© 2004 Sucker Punch Productions .

⊙ Go to `Tutorials/Chapter2` and copy the `Project_Character` directory to your hard drive. Open the file named `Character_Start.mb` in the directory's Scenes folder. In this file, you will find the image planes we will use as our guide for creating Silenus.

Creating Silenus's Head

The head can be the most difficult and complicated part of a character's body to model, but I encourage you to create the head first. It may be slow going, and you may find it a daunting task. But as you improve your modeling skills, even the most complicated model can eventually become second nature.

1. In the side view, create a polygon cylinder. Adjust its creation settings under the Inputs section of the Channel Box to 8 Subdivisions Axis and 1 Subdivisions Height. Move and scale it into position.

2. For the top of the head, create a polygonal sphere. Adjust its creation settings under the Inputs section of the Channel Box to 8 Subdivisions Axis and 8 Subdivisions Height. Scale it to closely match the size of the cylinder along the sphere's middle region (Figure 2.21).

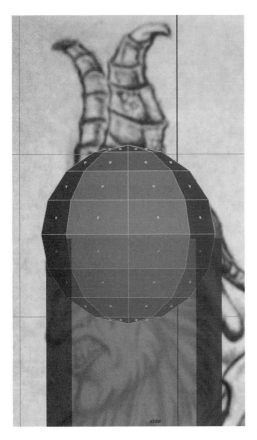

Figure 2.21 Create a sphere for the top of the head.

3. Delete all but the top two rows of faces and use the Snap to Point command (hold the V key) to snap the vertices along the sphere's opening to the opening on top of the cylinder. Select both objects, and use the Combine command under **Polygons > Combine**. Now, with both surfaces merged into one object, you can use the Merge Vertices command to merge the points along the opening, sealing the gaps.

4. Still in the side view, begin to move points around to fit the side profile of Silenus's head (Figure 2.22). Do the same for the front view.

Figure 2.22 Push and pull vertices around to match the concept.

5. To prepare the model for later mirroring, select half the faces and delete them.

The Nose

Now we need to work on Silenus's nose. His nose in particular is very angular and prominent and can be described as a major feature of his overall look. For such areas of interest, it is important to try to match the concept art as much as possible to convey the characteristics that the concept artist had in mind.

1. Using the Create Polygon tool in the side view, draw an outline of the overall nose shape and press Enter to create the surface (Figure 2.23).

2. Use the Extrude Face command to give the surface a thickness of about .06 units.

Figure 2.23 Use the Create Polygon tool to start the nose.

3. Using the Split Polygon tool, cut across the surface as shown in Figure 2.24. This will let us extrude the bottom part of the nose to create the nostrils.

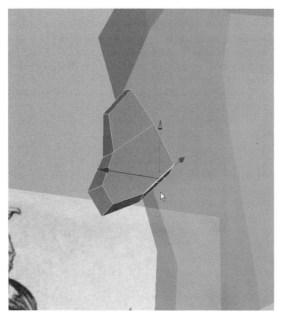

Figure 2.24 Cut across the surface.

4. Extrude the lower face to start the nostril approximately .08 units. Take this moment to push and pull the vertices around to more closely match the shape in the drawing.

5. Continue to split faces and adjust vertices, using the front and side view images as your guide (Figure 2.25).

Figure 2.25 Define the nose.

6. Use the Mirror command under **Polygons** > **Mirror Geometry** > **Options** to see what the nose looks like as a whole. In the options, choose the direction that your model needs to mirror across. In my case, it is -X. Make sure the faces where the two halves will meet are deleted.

7. Seeing the nose as one shape, we can start to adjust it as a whole to finish it up. In my case, I noticed that the tip of the nose needed to be tapered a little more and narrowed. Adjust your model's vertices and get it to a finished state (Figure 2.26).

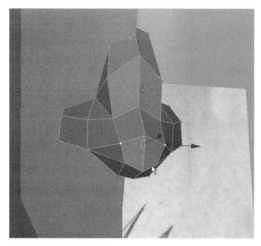

Figure 2.26 The finished nose

The Mouth

Now we can focus on the mouth. Obviously, for any sort of facial expression, the mouth is very important and needs to be able to articulate emotion and speech. Doing so is not too complicated, but can take practice.

1. Use the Split Polygon tool to create a V shape from the approximate corner of the mouth to top and bottom lip (Figure 2.27).

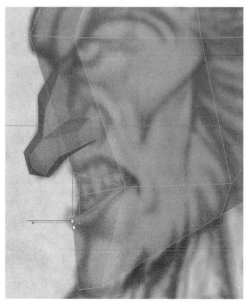

Figure 2.27 Begin cutting to form the mouth.

2. Split the middle of these faces and position the vertices to form the basic shape of the lips. Delete the face where the nose will blend into the head (Figure 2.28).

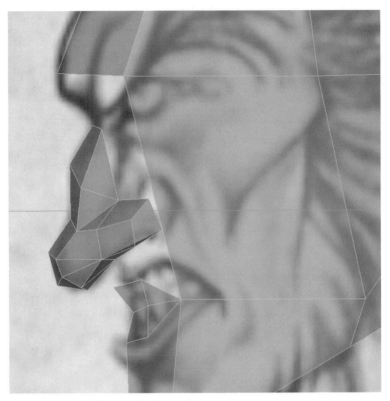

Figure 2.28 Delete the face impeding the nose.

3. Combine the surfaces of the head and the nose. Use the Append to Polygon tool to bridge the gap between the mouth and nose. Use the Split Polygon tool on the forehead to allow another append here, connecting the top of the nose to the forehead (Figure 2.29).

4. Under the mouth, use the Split Polygon tool to give more definition to the chin.

5. Use the Split Polygon tool to make a split diagonally from the upper corner of the mouth to the upper corner of the cheek. Click once in between to allow some definition of the angular cheekbones pictured in the drawing (Figure 2.30).

We want to append the gap to fill in the upper-right area above the mouth so that the mouth will articulate more realistically for speech and expression. So, we need to separate the lips and make the cavity for the mouth's interior.

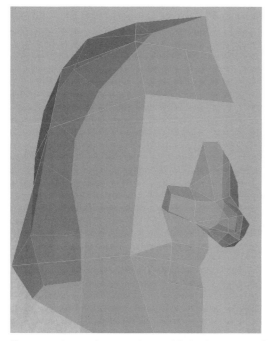

Figure 2.29 Connect the nose to the rest of the head.

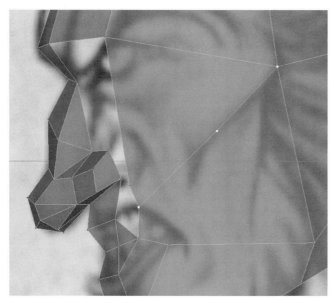

Figure 2.30 Create definition for the cheekbones.

6. Use a Bevel command on the edge where the lips should separate (Figure 2.31). You will probably need to adjust the bevel's Offset Distance attribute to about .2 to decrease the width of the resulting faces.

Figure 2.31 Use the Bevel command to create a gap.

7. Delete the new faces and merge the end vertex to the corner vertex of the mouth. We will also add new edges to add more definition (Figure 2.32).

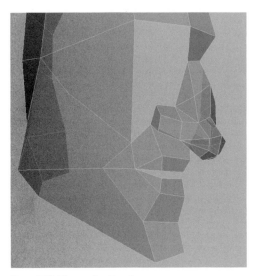

Figure 2.32 The mouth taking shape

8. Select the edges along the inner lips, and use the Extrude Edge command to extend geometry inward to start a cavity for the mouth interior.

9. Use the Append to Polygon tool to fill the gaps in between, and use the Split Polygon tool to cut across the middle. Pull these new edges back to create the entire cavity (for this half, anyway). However, the interior of the mouth is not an area that will be seen in much detail during gameplay, so we will use the Merge Vertices or Collapse command to clean up the geometry and optimize it as much as possible.

10. Adjust the vertices of the back of the jaw to define the curvature of the lower jaw and how it merges into the back of the head (Figure 2.33).

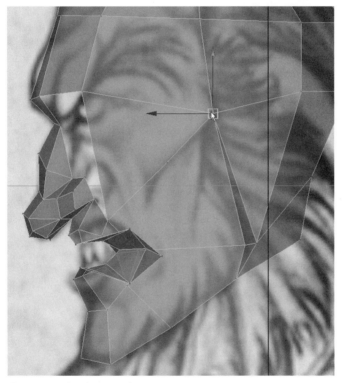

Figure 2.33 Define the rear jaw line.

For Silenus's teeth, we will use what is called *alpha transparency* or *opacity* in the textures. We will talk about that more in the next chapter. Essentially, we will create the teeth geometry as a flat surface and texture it with the teeth image later. It may look a little strange at the moment, but eventually it will work out.

11. For Silenus's teeth, use curved planes. Do the same for both the top and bottom teeth (Figure 2.34).

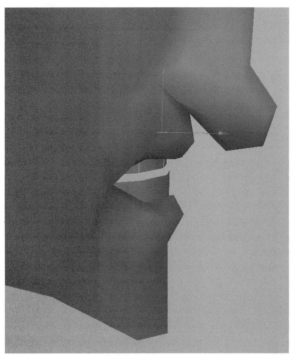

Figure 2.34 Get the planes in place for the teeth.

The Brow and Cheeks

Silenus has a very defined brow and cheek structure. These steps will walk through their creation.

1. For the brow of the character, delete the face covering the eye area. Select the edge above the eye area and use **Edit Polygons** > **Subdivide**. This will cut the edge in half, placing a new vertex at its center.

2. Use the Append to Polygon tool to fill the gap indicated in Figure 2.35. Adjust the vertices as shown.

3. Use the Split Polygon tool, and add definition to the forehead to start the distinctive hump you can see in the drawing between the two horns. Adjust the vertices, as you can see in Figure 2.36.

Figure 2.35 Defining the brow

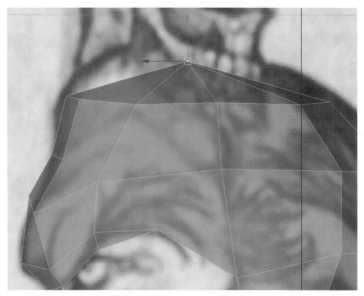

Figure 2.36 Creating the forehead hump

4. Split across the top of the head to round it a bit. Obviously, this results in some fairly unneeded geometry, so use the Collapse command to remove them (Figure 2.37).

Figure 2.37 Defining and cleaning up the forehead

5. Split a line vertically along the cheek to add definition. Use the Append to Polygon tool and fill in the large hole. Usually, it is easier to cut into geometry to form complex shapes than it is to construct them from scratch.

6. Split a line from the top of the nose to the nostril to help continue the line of the cheek. To define Silenus's sharp cheekbones, add a cut as pictured in Figure 2.38. Adjust the vertices to give it a defined shape.

The Eyes

Eyes can be very complicated. Learning to create them can take practice. First, you'll need to create the area for the eye, and then the eyeball itself.

1. Cut in a radial pattern around the eye by splitting polygons (Figure 2.39).

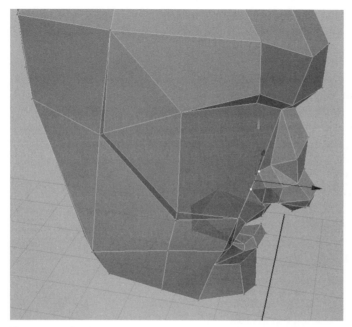

Figure 2.38 Define the cheekbones.

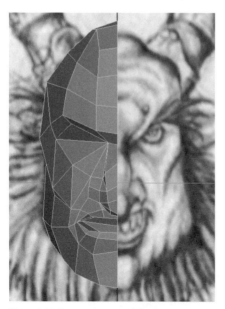

Figure 2.39 Start cutting around the eye.

2. To begin the actual eye socket, select the two triangular faces in the eye location. Using the Extrude Face command's scale tool, scale the extruded faces downward and delete the resulting faces (Figure 2.40).

Figure 2.40 Beginning the eye socket

3. Select the four edges around the eye socket, and use the Subdivide command to divide the edges into halves. With these new vertices, adjust them to create a more eye-like shape. Use the Split Polygon tool to create some radial cuts from these vertices to help round out the surrounding geometry (Figure 2.41).

    Before we go too much further, we need to create an actual eye around which to build the eyelid. No matter what shape the head of your project may be, in almost all cases, an eyeball is spherical and the eyelid needs to fit around it.

4. Create a polygon sphere and adjust its creation options under the Inputs section of the Channel Box to make the Subdivisions Axis and Height equal 8.

5. Using the image planes as your guide, position the sphere where the eye should go.

    Your eyelid probably doesn't look anything like what you want it to look. Adjusting what you have to fit around this ball and making it match the rest of the face can be the most difficult part of the eye modeling. You can experiment by making a few cuts and changes here and there, tweaking vertices as you go to adjust the shape. Add a new radial row of edges with the Split Polygon tool. Eventually, you can get something like Figure 2.42. Select the edges of the eyelid, and extrude them inward to create a small cavity to house the eye.

Figure 2.41 Adding geometry around the eye for further definition

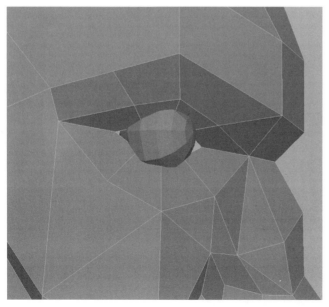

Figure 2.42 Place the sphere.

6. By using radial edges around the eye area (following the Edge Flow concept mentioned earlier) and cleaning up unneeded geometry, you can eventually create something similar to what is seen in Figure 2.43.

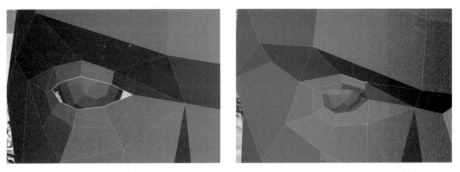

Figure 2.43 Assembling the eyelid

7. Because the eye's movement is fairly limited, we can delete the back quarter of the sphere.

The Beard

The beard will use the same technique as the teeth and is fairly simple to create.

1. Select the edges where the beard will meet the face, and extrude them out about 0.5 units. Adjust the vertices to fit the beard as guided by your images in the front and side views (Figure 2.44).

Figure 2.44 The beard geometry in place

2. To keep these large planes from constantly obstructing your view, select the faces and use **Edit Polygons > Extract** to make the beard plane its own object and hide it from view (Ctrl+H).

The Horns

For the horns, we will use an Extrude command that can be found under **Surfaces > Extrude**.

1. Use the CV Curve tool (**Create > CV Curve Tool**) in the front view, and trace the path of the horn.

2. In the side view, adjust the curve's CVs to fit that view as well.

3. Create a Nurbs Circle (**Create > NURBS Primitives > Circle**).

4. Using Snap to Curve, place the circle at the end of the horn as shown in Figure 2.45.

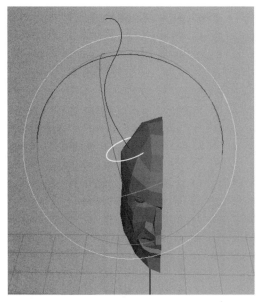

Figure 2.45 Place these curves to prepare to make the horn.

Note: Using Snap to Curve can be an exercise in frustration because it does not work as you might expect. With the C key pressed (or with Snap to Curve toggled in the Status line), hold the *middle* mouse button and click and drag on the curve. The object should snap to the curve every time.

5. Select the circle. Hold Shift and select the curve that makes up the path of the horn. With the two curves selected, go into the **Surfaces > Extrude > Options** and make the following changes:

- Change **Result Position** to **At Path**.
- Change **Pivot** to **Component**.

Changing the Result Position and Pivot options makes the resulting surface follow the path curve that runs along the horn.

- Change **Scale** to **0**.

Decreasing the Scale will taper the tip of the horn.

- Change **Output Geometry** to **Polygons**.

In the new options that appear, make the following choices:

- Change **Type** to **Quads**.
- Change **Tessellation Method** to **General**.
- Change **U Type** and **V Type** to **Per Span # of Iso Params**.
- Change **Number U** and **Number V** to **1**.

Changing the Output Geometry causes the command to create a polygon shape rather than its default NURBS (Non-Uniform Rational B-Spline) surface. By changing the output to Quads (we will triangulate it later) using the General Tessellation Method's options, we lower the amount of geometry to more game-like numbers.

If everything goes well, you should get something similar to Figure 2.46. Of course, if it is not exactly what you want, you can adjust the vertices to your liking. You will need to merge the vertices at the tip of the horns.

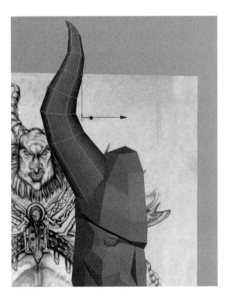

Figure 2.46 The horns in place

The Ears

The ears are relatively simple. Instead of creating the complicated ear interiors, we can simply texture them. From the perspective of most game cameras, such tiny details do not necessarily need to be modeled.

1. Create a cube with two divisions in the Width and Height.

2. Scale and position the cube to the approximate location of the ear, and pull the middle points on the end out for the ear's tip.

3. Adjust the vertices on top of the cube to form the folding shape of the ear, using the concept image as a guide. After some adjusting, you should eventually get something like the object in Figure 2.47.

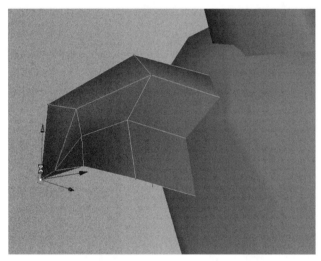

Figure 2.47 Creating the ear

Adding Finishing Touches

The head is almost complete. If you take another look at the side-view concept art, you can see that Silenus has a ponytail. Now, we do not want to go too far with it—we need to wait and see how the body works out so that we can make the ponytail drape realistically—but we can get it started.

In the back of the head, make a couple of cuts (Figure 2.48) with the Split Polygon tool. Grab the two edges on the end and use Extrude Edge. Do this a couple of times, positioning the vertices after each extrude. Use Flip Triangle Edge for the edges on the head to more closely follow the flow of the hair. The ponytail is not completed yet, but we are at a point where we can stop and come back later.

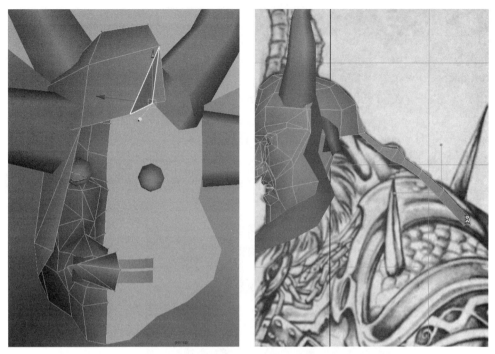

Figure 2.48 The ponytail taking shape

To see the head as a whole, we can use the Mirror Geometry (**Polygons > Mirror Geometry**) command. For pieces that are not halves (such as the ear, eye, and horn), you will need to use a different mirroring method.

1. Select the ear, eye, and horn objects, and press the Insert key on your keyboard. This allows you to edit the position of these objects' pivot point. Grid snap the pivot point to the center axis.

Note: To freeze objects into their current position and reset their channel information so that mirroring is easier, use **Modify > Freeze Transformations**.

2. Press Insert again to exit the Pivot editing mode, and duplicate your selected objects (**Edit > Duplicate**).

3. Freeze the duplicate's transformations (**Modify > Freeze Transformations**) to reset any channel information the geometry may have. To mirror the duplicates, enter -1 in the Scale X channel. (The direction you use may be different if your model is facing a different direction.)

You should get mirrored geometry on the other side of the head.

4. At this point, again freeze the geometry's transformations to make the negative value in the scale channel positive. Reverse the duplicate's normals (**Edit Polygons > Normals > Reverse**). Select both halves and combine (**Polygons > Combine**) them together.

Normals represent the geometry's surface direction. When combining objects together, you want to make certain the normals of the geometry in question are facing the same direction. This keeps the rendering of both objects consistent in Maya as well as in the game.

Note: To view an object's normals, select it, and go to **Display > Polygon Components > Normals**. Use this command a second time to hide them.

5. Merge the vertices where the two halves meet.

Congratulations! The head is finally done (Figure 2.49). You just finished the most complicated part of modeling a character. Now let's see about tackling the rest of him.

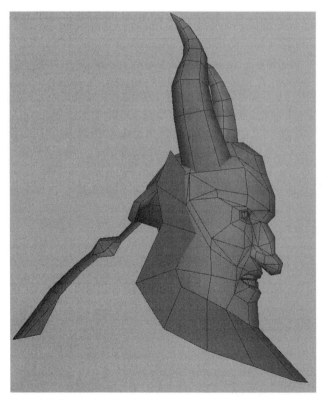

Figure 2.49 The completed head

Creating Silenus's Body

The hard part is out of the way, so now we can concentrate on Silenus's body. At first, we will ignore the clothing that he is wearing and concentrate on just getting his body formed. Then, we will go back and adorn him with his warrior garb.

The Torso

First, we need to create a layer to put our finished head in so that we can keep everything organized. This will allow us to hide the head while we work on the body. After the head is hidden, we can create Silenus's body.

1. The Layer Bar is under the Channel Box at the bottom right of the screen. Here, click the Create a New Layer button to create a new layer. Select the head geometry, and right-click on Layer 2. Choose Add Selected Objects. Click on the V icon next to the layer name to turn off the visibility, effectively hiding the head geometry.

2. To start the torso, create a polygonal cylinder and scale and position it accordingly. Adjust the creation options under the Inputs in the Channel Box:

   - Subdivisions Axis: 8
   - Subdivisions Height: 4
   - Subdivisions Caps: 0

3. Adjust rows of vertices to match the concept in both the front and side views. Keep in mind the concept of Edge Flow, and follow the contours of the body with the geometry (Figure 2.50). Once you get a good basic shape, you can delete half of the body.

Figure 2.50 Adjusting the vertices

4. Start using the Split Polygon tool to add definition to the belly and back and a new row of vertices for the neck area (Figure 2.51).

Figure 2.51 Adding definition

5. Using the Split Polygon tool, form the shape of Silenus's chest as seen in the concepts (Figure 2.52).

Note: An *instance* of your geometry is a duplicate that will also copy whatever changes you make to the original.

6. Select the torso geometry that we have so far, and use **Edit > Duplicate > Options**. Select Instance next to Geometry Type. In the first Scale column (the three columns represent X, Y, and Z, so the first column would be the X direction), input -1. When you hit the duplicate button, the torso should mirror across the X direction and mimic any changes you make from now on.

7. Continue defining the torso using the Split Polygon Tool, and adjust the vertices to form the shape of Silenus's body. Use the concept art as your guide (Figure 2.53).

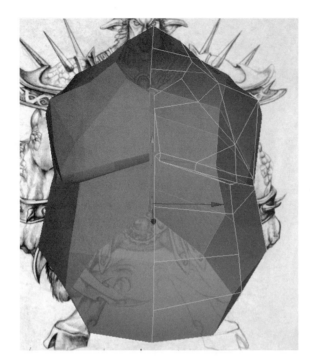

Figure 2.52 Shaping the chest and using an instance

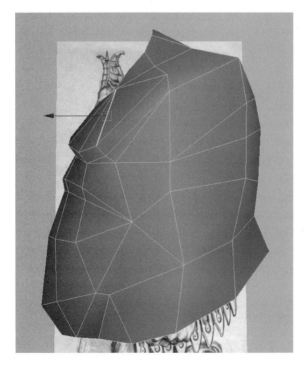

Figure 2.53 Adding more definition

The Legs

Silenus is a satyr, a race of mythical creatures that are half man, half goat. As such, his legs do not follow the typical human structure. This can make the legs a little more complicated than usual.

1. To start the leg, create a cylinder. Use the same creation options as we did with the torso except with a Subdivisions Height of 3. Scale and position the cylinder in place. Adjust the vertices to form the upper leg (Figure 2.54).

> **Note:** The 3D model may need to be repositioned to make it work properly. Occasionally, in cases such as Silenus's leg, you may find that the structures depicted in a 2D drawing do not necessarily work correctly in 3D space.

Figure 2.54 The leg beginning to take shape

2. Select the face at the bottom of the leg. Right-click on the surface, select Edge as the component type, and hold the Shift key to add the adjacent edge to your selection. With both the face *and* the edge selected, perform a Wedge Faces command (**Edit Polygons > Wedge Faces**). Adjust the wedge angle to 90 degrees and the divisions to 3 in the Channel Box Inputs section (Figure 2.55).

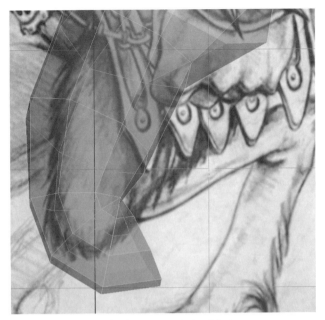

Figure 2.55 Using the Wedge Faces command to bend the leg geometry

You may notice that this forms a V-shaped edge formation at this joint. This will give this area better articulation for future animation.

3.   Use Extrude Face to extend the leg out about 1.5 units as in Figure 2.56.

Figure 2.56 Extrude the faces to extend the leg further.

4. To create the long "foot," create a new cylinder with the same prior creation options in the Channel Box Inputs section and position and scale it accordingly. Select both objects, and combine them (**Polygons > Combine**). Now use the Merge Vertices command at the seam (Figure 2.57).

> **Note:** To avoid having to input the same numbers into the Channel Box Inputs over and over again, you can input these numbers into the options under **Create > Polygon Primitives > Cylinder > Options**. Afterward, each additional cylinder you create will keep the set options.

Figure 2.57 Combine and merge the two objects.

5. Use the Append to Polygon tool to fill in the remaining gap. Use the Split Polygon tool to cut these new faces in half, and position the vertices to round out the joint.

6. Use the Extrude Face command to extend this new part of the leg about 1 unit to begin to form the hoof.

7. Split some edges into the middle of the hoof to form the separated halves.

The Arms

We will come back to the legs so that we can attach them to the body. For now, let's go ahead and start the arms. We will hide the body for the moment.

1. Create a polygon cylinder. Scale and position it using the orthographic views. Adjust its creation options to take the subdivisions caps to 0, height to 3, and axis to 8. Adjust the vertices to start forming the shape of the arm (Figure 2.58).

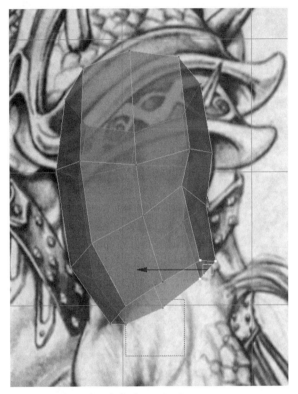

Figure 2.58 Placing the cylinder for starting the arm

2. Use the Split Polygon tool to add more definition to the arm. Grab the bottom row of edges, and use Extrude Edge to extend the geometry to begin the forearm. Use the concept art as your guide (Figure 2.59).

3. Extrude the edges again about 0.5 units. Adjust the vertices using your front and side views as your guide.

Once again, you may not be able to adhere strictly to the drawing to ensure the shapes make sense in 3D space. Using anatomy references can be a big help.

4. Split a couple of edges at the elbow to form a V-joint (Figure 2.60).

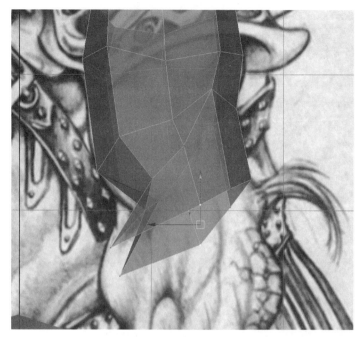

Figure 2.59 Extruding down the forearm

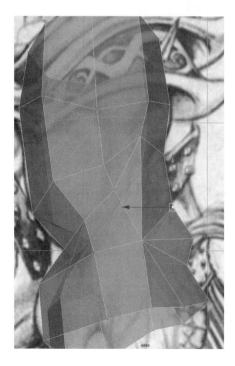

Figure 2.60 Creating a V-joint at the elbow

5. Extrude the edges once again about 0.5 units to extend the arm geometry to the wrist.

6. Use the Split Polygon tool to add definition to the triceps and bicep muscles (Figure 2.61).

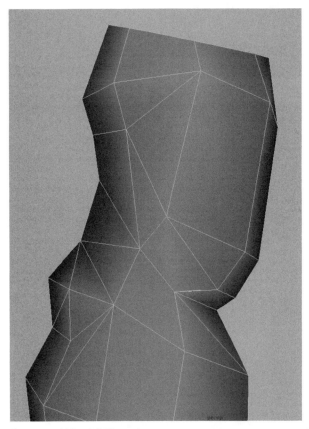

Figure 2.61 Adding definition to the upper arm

The shoulder area is hidden under the shoulder pads. Because the area will always be hidden, we can be a little less strict with the shoulder's shape and not worry as much about anatomical accuracy. In a real game situation, however, the character could change costume through the course of the game, so keep that in mind.

7. Grab the edges at the top of the arm, and use the Extrude Edge command a couple of times to initiate the shape (Figure 2.62).

8. Use the Split Polygon tool to add some definition, and use the Append to Polygon tool to fill in some of the gaps (Figure 2.63).

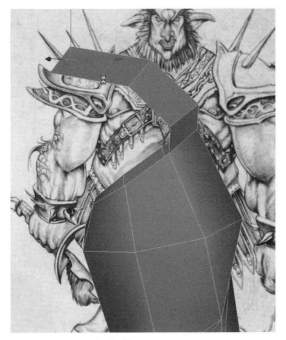

Figure 2.62 Starting the shoulder

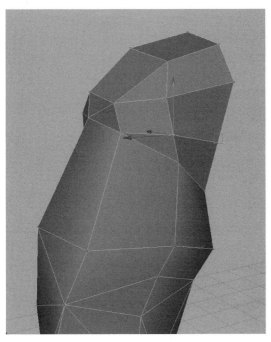

Figure 2.63 Finishing up the shoulder's shape

The Hands

The hands are another complicated part of a character's body that will take some practice to perfect because of the many fingers branching from the hand's structure. Forming a shape that can accommodate the fingers as well as fit into the wrist can be quite a challenge.

1. Create a polygon cylinder, scale, and position it at the wrist.

    The Cut Faces tool is like an auto-split function that will make a division throughout the model in a designated straight line. You will probably want to use an orthographic view, such as the side view, when using this tool.

2. Select the **Edit Polygons > Cut Faces Tool**. In the side view, click and drag on the model to project a line through the geometry based on your camera view. Adjust the vertices, and use the Split Polygon tool to begin forming the palm (Figure 2.64).

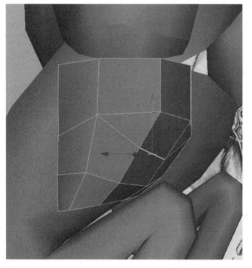

Figure 2.64 The hand taking shape

Creating the Fingers

1. Create another cylinder for the fingers. Scale and position it at the end of the palm. Use the Split Polygon tool to add a V-joint to the finger's knuckle. Extrude the faces to extend the finger about 1 unit (Figure 2.65).

2. Use the Split Polygon tool to cut into the edges for the fingernail, and adjust the vertices to extend it from the finger's main shaft.

3. Duplicate the finger, and adjust the scale to make the four fingers of the hand (Figure 2.66).

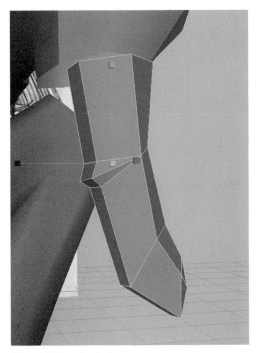

Figure 2.65 Creating the finger

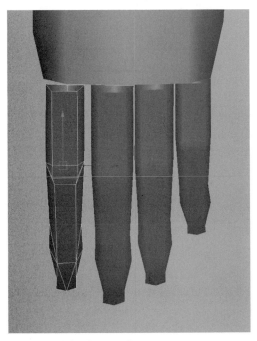

Figure 2.66 All four fingers in place

4. Use **Polygons** > **Combine** to join the four fingers and the hand. Split some geometry into the hand so that the edges of the hand meet the edges of the fingers. Using Merge Vertices and the Append to Polygon tool, merge the fingers into the hand (Figure 2.67).

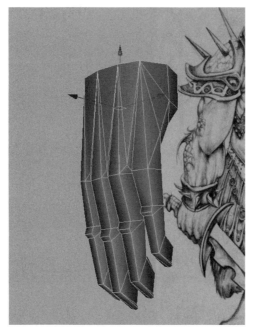

Figure 2.67 The fingers attached to the hand

Shaping the Hand and Attaching It

Now that we have a good shape for the basic hand, we can use a Lattice deformer (**Deform** > **Create Lattice** under the Animation module) to shape it into the big, burly hand of Silenus, as depicted in the drawing (Figure 2.68).

Note: A lattice allows you to modify the overall shape of a model using fewer points placed on a 3D grid. To adjust the number of divisions in the grid, use the Shape options in the Channel Box.

1. To create the thumb, select the faces of one of the fingers and use the Duplicate Face command under **Edit Polygons** > **Duplicate Face**. This will create a new object, duplicating the selected faces.

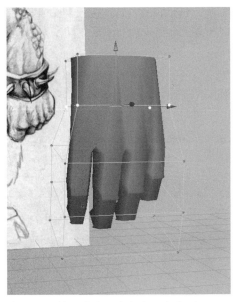

Figure 2.68 Using a lattice to help shape the hand

2. Position this new duplicate in the approximate thumb position, and use the Combine command to combine the two into one object. Use the Merge Vertices command and the Append to Polygon tool to fill in the gaps (Figure 2.69).

Figure 2.69 The thumb in place

3. Position the hand in relation to the arm. Combine the arm and hand together. Use the Merge Vertices command to fill in the gaps (Figure 2.70).

The arm's elbow is to the back, so we need to rotate the hand so that the palm is facing more toward the front. Stretch your own arm out and take a look at where the elbow is in relation to the twist of your forearm.

Note: Observe the way your body moves. Stretch your arms and legs. Twist your wrists, elbows, and ankles. Try to mimic the way your joints work when you create joints in your characters. Doing so will make them more realistic.

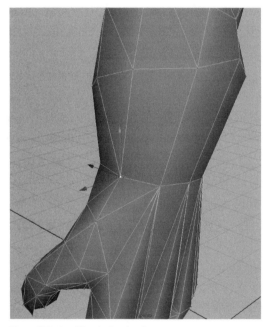

Figure 2.70 Attaching the hand to the arm

4. To help the articulation of the wrist, use the Cut Faces tool to add a new row of edges between the wrist and forearm.

Putting It All Together

Now that the arm and hand are together, we can start to merge the arm into the body. Press the Insert key, and move the pivot to the shoulder. Rotate the arm about 20 to 25 degrees, as shown in Figure 2.71.

1. To prepare the torso for the arm, select the faces depicted in Figure 2.72 and delete them. This will leave a hole for the arm.

Figure 2.71 Rotate the arm.

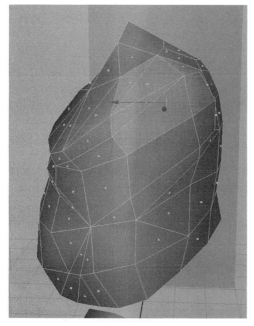

Figure 2.72 Delete faces on the torso to make room for the arm.

2. Combine the torso and arm, and use Merge Vertices to fill the gaps.

3. Combine the leg to the torso. Use the Append to Polygon tool to create a connection between the front and back of the pelvis (Figure 2.73).

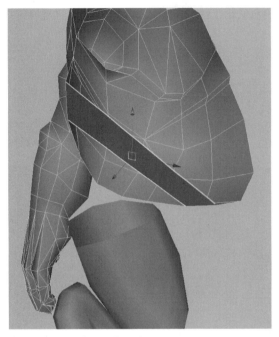

Figure 2.73 Append across the groin.

4. Select both edges of the newly created face, and use **Edit Polygons > Subdivide > Options**. Under Options, increase the Subdivision Levels to 4, and click Apply and Close. Use the Split Polygon tool to create the divisions between these new vertices.

5. Combine the two objects, and use the Append to Polygon tool and Merge Vertices command to blend them together (Figure 2.74).

We have now successfully formed half of the body. Delete any instanced duplicates you may have. Make a standard duplicate of the body (reset the duplicate options), and mirror it using the negative scale method. Combine the two halves, and use Merge Vertices to make the body one object.

6. Unhide the head layer. Adjust the ponytail to drape realistically over the back of the body.

7. Hide the beard plane for now. Combine the head and the body. Use the Append to Polygon tool to fill in the gaps (Figure 2.75).

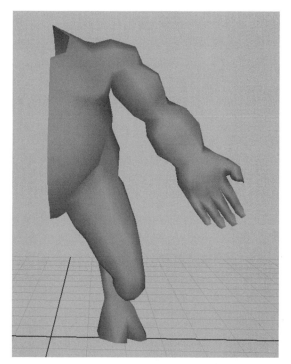

Figure 2.74 The leg connected to the body

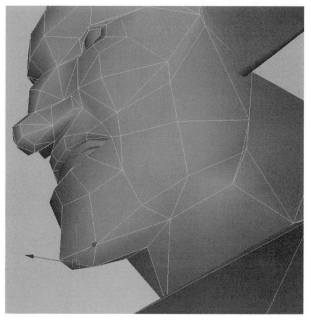

Figure 2.75 The head attached

Creating Silenus's Armor

Now it is time to fit Silenus with his gear. We will start easy and begin his wristbands.

1. Create a cylinder and adjust the creation options under the Channel Box's Inputs section:

- Subdivisions Axis: 8
- Subdivisions Height: 2
- Subdivisions Caps: 0

2. Scale and position the cylinder on the wrist.

3. Extrude and scale the two faces on the cap to round the edges of the wristband (Figure 2.76).

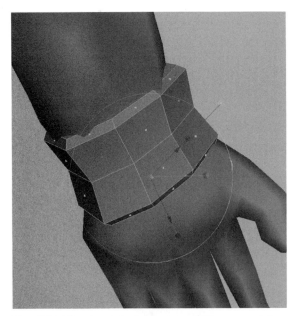

Figure 2.76 Adjust the wristband geometry to be a bit more rounded.

Keep your polycount in mind when you add these types of details. During the cleanup phase of creation, you will probably discover that the small polygons used to round the wristband edges need to be removed to fit under the poly limit. But for now, go ahead and add the geometry you see fit.

4. For the wristband spikes, create a polygonal cone and adjust the creation options as follows:

- Subdivisions Axis: 3
- Subdivisions Height: 3
- Subdivisions Caps: 0

As depicted in the concept image, the spikes need to be curved. Rather than doing this by hand, we can use the Nonlinear Bend deformer. With the spike selected, use **Deform** > **Create Nonlinear** > **Bend** from the Animation module (F2). Adjust the Curvature option in the bend deformer's Inputs in the Channel Box to about 1 (Figure 2.77). Make sure the spike is selected, and delete its history under **Edit** > **Delete by Type** > **History**. This will *bake* (or "make permanent") the deformer's effects into the geometry.

Figure 2.77 Creating a spike

5. Position and duplicate the spike to create the rest of them. Rotate each spike so that they are not all curved in the same direction.

The Belts

To create the belt, we use the Make Live command. This allows you to use a model as a grid upon which you can create.

1. Select the body, and go to **Modify** > **Make Live**. The model will turn into a green wireframe. Using **Create** > **CV Curve Tool**, click on the model to create the points for the curve, as depicted in Figure 2.78. Continue around to the middle of the back. Use Grid Snap to make sure the CV (control vertex) on the end of the curve is snapped to the center axis of the grid.

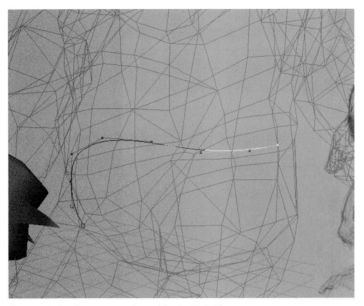

Figure 2.78 Creating a curve on the model using Make Live

2. Duplicate the curve. You may need to reset the duplicate command's options under **Edit > Duplicate > Options**. In the option box that opens, go to **Edit > Reset Settings**. Move the newly duplicated curve up above the original about 0.25 units.

3. Use the **Surfaces > Loft** command with polygonal outputs (see step 5 in "The Horns" section for the polygonal output settings) to create the belt geometry.

Note: If you need more geometry, increase the U or V Number options of the Loft as you see fit.

Extrude the faces of the belt about 0.075 units to give the belt thickness. Because the faces on the interior of the belt will be hidden by the body, delete them (Figure 2.79).

4. Duplicate and mirror the belt half. Combine and merge the two halves into one.

5. To create the large belt emblem, create another cylinder. Rotate it so the cap faces the front, and scale and position the cylinder as in Figure 2.80.

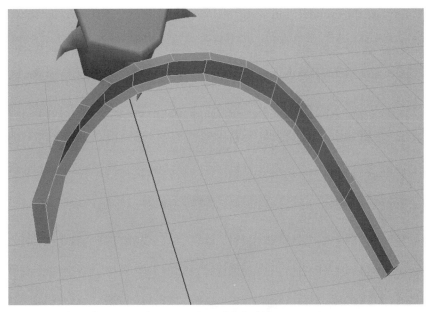

Figure 2.79 Loft a surface between the curves, and extrude it for thickness.

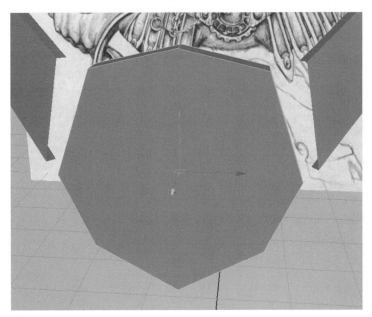

Figure 2.80 Creating the belt buckle

6. Duplicate the cylinder, and scale the front face to form the jewel-like structure on the front of the buckle. Combine the buckle to the belt, and use Merge Vertices to fill in the gaps.

7. Use the Make Live command to draw a new curve for the straps on the upper torso.

8. Use the same steps as with the belt. Duplicate the curve and loft between them. Extrude the faces to give the strap thickness, and delete the hidden faces. Duplicate and mirror the strap for the other side; combine and merge them together (Figure 2.81).

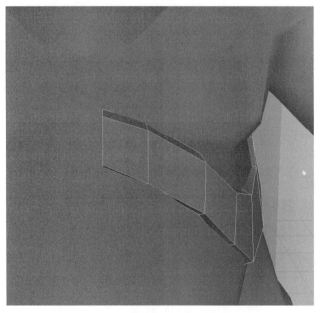

Figure 2.81 Using the same method for the belt as for the straps

9. If you haven't already done so, you can mirror the wristband created earlier for the other side of the model.

10. Use a cube to create the buckle in the middle of the strap, and use planes for the small hanging pieces of leather (Figure 2.82).

The Kilt and Shoulder Pads

As with the teeth and beard, the kilt will use their texture to add detail. As such, we will create simple planes for now.

1. Create planes for the kilt slats, and position them around the belt (Figure 2.83).

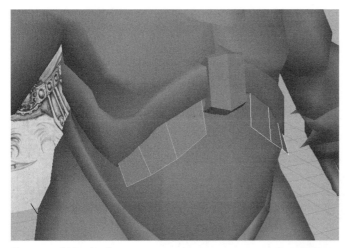

Figure 2.82 Adding details

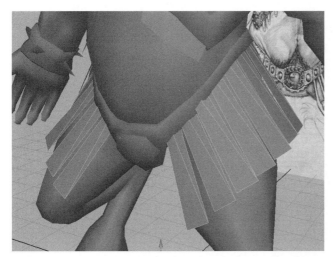

Figure 2.83 Creating the kilt

2. For the shoulder pads, create a cylinder. Rotate the cylinder 90 degrees so the caps are facing to the side. Delete the caps and the two bottom faces. Scale and position the cylinder on the shoulder, and start adjusting the vertices to fit the shape (Figure 2.84).

3. Use the Append to Polygon tool to fill in the front end, and use the Split Polygon tool to split it down the middle to create more geometry for further definition (Figure 2.85).

4. Use the Append to Polygon tool to fill in the gaps on the underside of the shoulder pad.

Figure 2.84 Starting the shoulder pads

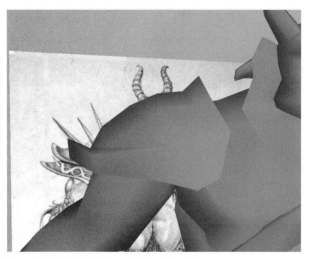

Figure 2.85 Adding definition to the shoulder pads

The underside of the shoulder pad is very visible from many directions. Depending on the game engine that your game project uses, the pads may not render when you look at the underside of the geometry. We will prevent this by filling in these gaps. The underside of the pads are rarely seen, however, so we can use the Collapse command to decrease the amount of their geometry to more manageable levels.

5. Duplicate and mirror the shoulder pad to the other side, and create three-sided polygon cones for the spikes. Delete the faces on their underside, as they will be hidden from view.

6. Create a polygonal sphere, and delete half of it. Place it on the chest for the chest piece jewel depicted in the drawing (Figure 2.86).

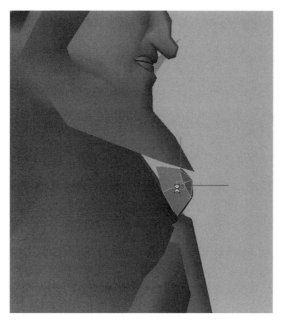

Figure 2.86 Setting the chest jewel in place

Cleanup

At this point, we should import the sword we created earlier so that we can get a better look at the polycount we have so far and adjust its size to fit the character. I scaled the sword about 75 percent larger. Obviously, your results may vary. I have accumulated 3649 polygons, a bit over my limit of 3500. You are probably over the limit too. So now we need to do some cleaning up.

We will start the cleanup process by going to the least important parts of the model and seeing what we can do to get rid of some of the geometry there. First, let's look at the sword. The sword's handle has a lot of faces that are not necessarily required—especially considering that Silenus's hand will be covering most of it. We can use the Collapse command to decrease it substantially. This technique brought my polycount down to 3581, so I am almost there.

Next, let's take a look at the spikes on the wristband and remove one of the divisions in each. We can also remove the slight bevel that the wristbands have on their rounded edges (Figure 2.87). That did the trick for me. I am now down to 3457, which will leave me enough room to add a few more details. Continue working with your model until your polycounts are within bounds.

Figure 2.87 The wristbands after minimizing their geometry

Adding Final Details

In the concept image, Silenus has a few tufts of hair on his legs and elbows, and he has some rather bushy eyebrows. Similarly to the way we created the beard, we will position polygonal planes for later texturing using alpha transparency (Figure 2.88).

Figure 2.88 Planes for the hair tufts

I have enough room in my polycount to create the secondary shoulder pad that you can see below the main piece of armor in the concept image. We will create it using the same method we used to create the primary should pad, using a cylinder and manipulating the points into something similar to Figure 2.89.

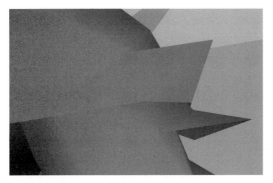

Figure 2.89 Adding the second shoulder pad layer

Congratulations! You have completed the model of Silenus, the Satyr Warrior. Feel free at this point to continue the model to a further state. You may notice that I did not model the tunic that is draped over Silenus's upper chest and shoulders. That detail will be incorporated into the texture. However, you may feel free to go further in the cleanup process to free up more polygons to use as you see fit. You might even try using a higher polygon limit for your own project.

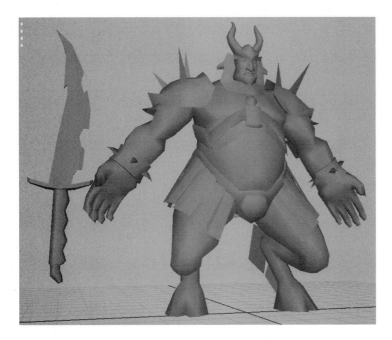

Texturing

To bring life to your model, you must texture it. In the gaming world, it's often best to do your texturing before you rig and animate your model. The main process you need to be aware of is what is known as UV Mapping. This process will allow you to make a 2D image that will wrap around a 3D object and display the image where you want to display it. Texturing is really what makes or breaks a model's believability, especially when you have low polygon limits. You can have a great model, but if your texture is mediocre, it can really hurt your model's overall quality. On the other hand, even a lower-quality model can look great with a high-quality texture.

Chapter Contents

Texturing in the Gaming World

History is the record of your actions that Maya keeps for your scene. Because of the memory this history can take, it is efficient to delete the history that is no longer required as your scene progresses. Both processes of UV Mapping and rigging can add a lot of history to an object. However, because the history created by rigging a character is required for the rigging to function, I recommend going through the process of UV Mapping and texturing your model first. This way, you can remove the unnecessary history resulting from UV Mapping before you begin the rigging process. Once a character has been bound to a skeleton, deleting the history is no longer an option. More about rigging will be discussed in the following chapter.

However, you must apply and lay out your model's UV coordinates before you can assign your textures.

Mapping UVs

Just as 3D space is described using X, Y, and Z to indicate the three dimensions of width, height, and depth, textures in 2D space are described using U and V for width and height. UVs are indicated using points. In the case of polygons, each vertex of a polygonal mesh is capable of holding a coordinate for use in texturing. This is a UV.

If you create a polygonal cube primitive from the Create menu, it is automatically mapped with UV coordinates. To see these UVs, select the cube and go to **Window > UV Texture Editor**. A window will appear as in Figure 3.1. In this window, you will manipulate the layout of your UVs for texture preparation. With a cube selected, you see the six faces laid out clearly. Every primitive comes with a set of default texture coordinates.

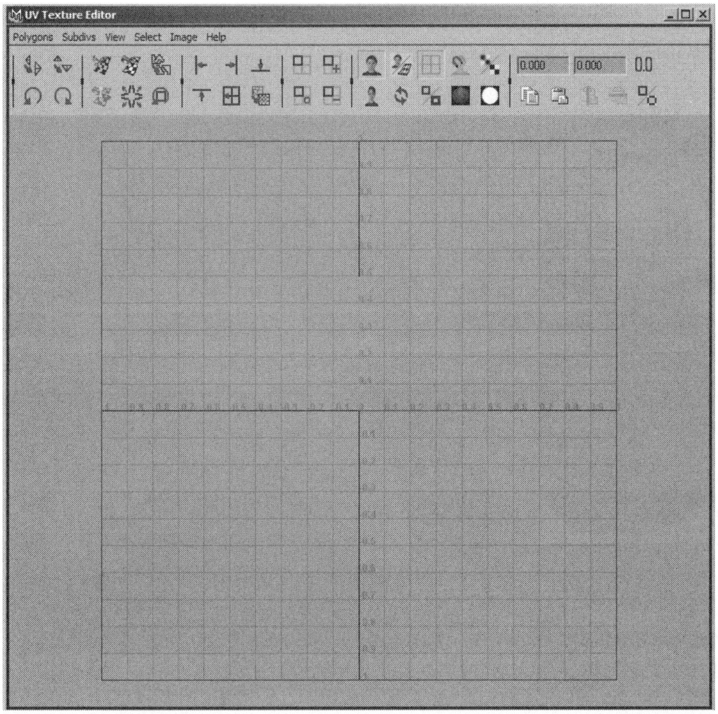

Figure 3.1 The UV Texture Editor

However, if you were to select Silenus's mesh and look in the UV Texture Editor window, you might find nothing or, more likely, a tangled mess of UVs crisscrossing all over the place. How do you to alleviate this? That is where UV Mapping comes into play. Under the **Edit Polygons > Texture** menu, you will find quite a few options, all having to do with UV projecting, mapping, and editing. Many of these options can also be found in the control panel of the UV Texture Editor window. Before you learn more about UV Mapping, you need to understand the different kinds of UV projection tools.

Note: Make sure that **Edit Polygons > Texture > Assign Shader to Each Projection** is unchecked. This option will assign a new material to each projection you make, which you do not need as it will create an unnecessary number of materials in your scene.

Maya in Games: Metroid Prime

Genre Sci-Fi Action Adventure

Developer Retro Studios

Publisher Nintendo

Platform Nintendo Gamecube

Metroid Prime is a fantastic First-Person Shooter (FPS) for the Gamecube. The character modeling is superb, but the environments are breathtaking in their immersive details. The game engine renders everything perfectly with fantastic lighting.

You cannot go wrong with Metroid's graphics. The artists definitely knew what they were doing, and it shows brilliantly. I highly recommend technical study of this game primarily for the environment modeling and particle effects, as well as the very well done textures.

You play Samus, a character that fans of the series will remember from the previous Metroid games. Using a plethora of well-modeled and animated weapons and special attacks, you battle lots of different aliens and monsters on your way through the story toward a classic confrontation at the end. Has Mother Brain from the previous games returned? That is only one of the mysteries you will have to uncover.

UV Projection Commands

Using the UV projection commands is relatively straightforward; however, understanding how to apply the commands in different situations might take some time. Familiarity will come with practice and time. The purpose of the commands is to select groups of faces and project new UV coordinates onto them that can then be maneuvered in the UV Texture Editor. With that in mind, we will now go over the different options available to use. The projection commands include:

Planar Mapping (Edit Polygons > Texture > Planar Mapping) Planar Mapping will project UVs onto the selected faces from a 3D projection object in the shape of a flat plane (Figure 3.2). In the projection options, the direction of the planar projection can be set to one of the orthographic directions (X, Y, or Z), or it can be projected from the angle of your camera.

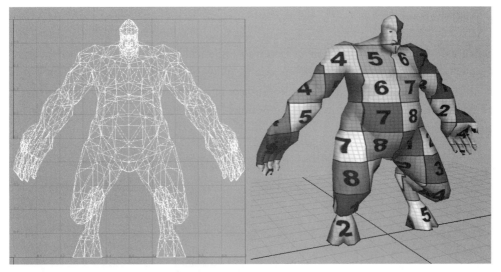

Figure 3.2 Planar Mapping projects UVs on the selected geometry from a flat plane. Shown here are the UV result (left) and the texture result (right).

Cylindrical Mapping (Edit Polygons > Texture > Cylindrical Mapping) Cylindrical Mapping will project UVs onto the selected faces from a 3D projection object in the shape of a cylinder (Figure 3.3). Obviously, this is most useful for objects of a cylindrical shape. In the options found in the Channel Box, you can adjust how much of a full cylinder is projected.

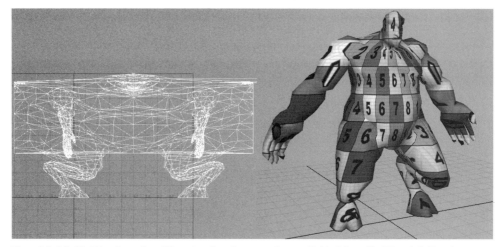

Figure 3.3 Cylindrical Mapping projects UVs on the selected geometry from a cylindrical shape. The UV result (left) and texture result (right) are shown.

Spherical Mapping (Edit Polygons > Texture > Spherical Mapping) The projection results from Spherical Mapping are, as you would expect, useful for sphere-shaped objects. As with the rest, a 3D projection object in the shape of a sphere will be created (Figure 3.4). You can adjust its creation options to determine the angle of projection around the object.

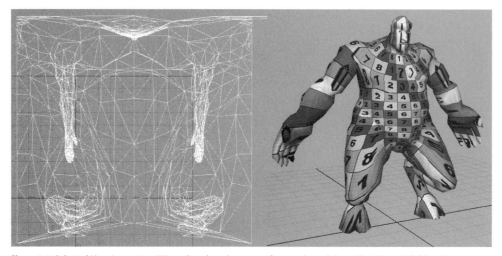

Figure 3.4 Spherical Mapping projects UVs on the selected geometry from a spherical shape. The UV result (left) and texture result (right) are shown.

Automatic Mapping (Edit Polygons > Texture > Automatic Mapping) Contrary to the previous projection commands, Automatic Mapping will try to map the selected geometry as cleanly as possible without using any sort of 3D objects from which to project. This command will divide the selected faces based on an angle and the number of projection directions you determine in the options, and then it will planar map them. It will then lay them out straight (Figure 3.5). This can be handy for irregularly shaped objects.

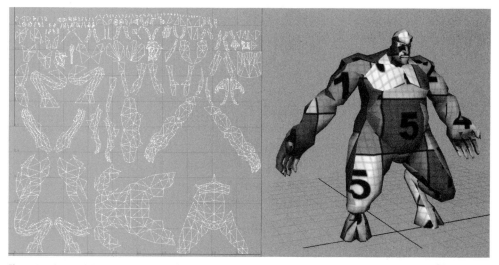

Figure 3.5 Automatic Mapping projects UVs from multiple directions to unwrap the selected geometry. The UV result (left) and texture result (right) are shown.

I like to use the Automatic Mapping projection command for most organic shapes. However, projecting the UVs is not the only step involved in readying a piece of geometry for texturing. UV Projection is only the first step in the process. There is still a matter of efficiently laying out these UVs. That is where the UV Texture Editor comes into use. Using the commands in the UV Texture Editor control panel, you can adjust and rearrange the projected UVs to lay out as efficiently as possible within the upper-right grid square of the visible area. The upper-right part of the grid is where your textures will be placed (Figure 3.6). This is part of the process that will come more easily with practice.

Figure 3.6 A UV layout in place in the UV Texture Editor

The UV Texture Editor

The UV Texture Editor (**Window > UV Texture Editor**) is where you perform the sometimes-tedious action of arranging your UV layout. Let's go over some of the more common commands found in the UV Texture Editor toolbar and menus.

Flip UVs (UV Texture Editor > Polygons > Flip UVs) This command will flip a group of selected UVs 180 degrees in either the U or V directions.

Rotate UVs (UV Texture Editor > Polygons > Rotate UVs) This command will rotate a group of selected UVs 45 degrees in either the U or V direction.

Align UVs (UV Texture Editor > Polygons > Align UVs) The Align UVs button allows you to align the selected UVs in a row, using the maximum or minimum value in the U or V direction as the value to which you align.

Cut UVs (UV Texture Editor > Polygons > Cut UVs) The Cut UVs command will separate the UVs of the selected edge(s).

Sew UVs (UV Texture Editor > Polygons > Sew UVs) The Sew UVs is the opposite of Cut UVs and will merge the UVs of the selected adjacent edge(s).

Move and Sew UVs (UV Texture Editor > Polygons > Move and Sew UVs) This is the same as the Sew UVs command, except it will move the entire UV shell of the selected edge instead of stretching the UVs across the editor when the merging edges are not close to each other in the editor. A *UV Shell* is a grouping of UVs in the UV Texture Editor.

UV Snapshot (UV Texture Editor > Polygons > UV Snapshot) The UV Snapshot command is what you will use once your UV layout is complete. It will save an image of your UV layout to use in a paint program, such as Photoshop, as a guide for your texture. The options allow you to set the file format and resolution of the image that is created.

Texture Resolutions and Formats

Deciding what resolution (height and width) and file format to use for the texture in your project is important. A variety of factors can influence your decisions.

The first thing to realize is that texture resolutions must be in what is known as a *Power of Two*. The more common texture resolutions are as follows:

- 64×64
- 128×128
- 256×256
- 512×512
- 1024×1024

Game consoles have a very limited amount of texture memory compared to computers; therefore, smaller resolutions are generally used. For example, a single character model created for a particular Playstation2 game required the use of three textures—two 256×256 textures for the body and one 64×64 texture for the head. On the other hand, characters created for a PC game I was involved with used one or possibly two 512×512 textures each. Your Art Director and programming team will tell you what kind of texture limitations your project will have.

When creating your textures, you should create the texture larger than you actually need for your project. This will allow you to pack more detail into the image, and it will give you the ability to use a variety of different texture resolutions from the larger source file when creating a game for multiple platforms with different resolution requirements. I generally recommend creating a texture one Power of Two larger than the maximum file resolution. If your game will use a 512×512 texture, create the texture at 1024×1024 and shrink the image upon completion.

For our Silenus project, we will use one 512×512 for the body, one 256×256 for the head, and one 256×256 for the sword. When creating the textures, we will use one Power of Two larger (one 1024×1024 and two 512×512).

Many image formats are available in the UV Snapshot options; however, you probably will want to use either Targa (.tga) or TIFF (.tif) formats because they keep alpha channel information and they are frequently used in modern game engines. For our project, we will use .tga. Either format will work just fine.

Alpha Channel and Pixel Shader Effects

Your standard game texture is an RGB image (using Red, Green, and Blue channels). Adding a fourth channel creates what is called an *alpha channel*. This extra channel holds secondary texture information in the form of a grayscale image that can be used in a variety of ways depending on the game engine. Alpha channels are most commonly used for the following:

Opacity/Transparency This is probably the most common use of an alpha channel. In the alpha, wherever the alpha is white, the model will be opaque; wherever the alpha is black, the model will be transparent.

Specularity This is another very common use of an alpha channel in games. Wherever the alpha is white, the model will be highly specular or shiny; wherever the alpha is black, the model will have no specularity.

Incandescence Not quite as common is the use of an alpha channel for incandescence, which will create a glow effect where the alpha is white.

Reflectivity Similar to Specularity, except instead of a simple white specular highlight where the alpha is white, the model will reflect a created reflectivity texture map. The reflectivity map is usually a Cube Map, which is a type of texture that is used by the game engine to project an image from all around the model. This type of map is used mostly for reflectivity as you project sky from above, trees and buildings from the sides, and grass or dirt from the floor. These are created in a variety of ways, and your project director should be able to let you know how your particular job handles it.

Other alpha channel effects are commonly used in the case of pixel shaders, which are becoming much more prevalent in modern games. Pixel shaders have special render effects on a per-pixel basis on the model, as opposed to the more common per-vertex method that had been used previously. Arguably, the most dramatic pixel shader effect is the use of bump maps and normal maps.

Bump Maps and Normal Maps Bump maps and normal maps are very similar in purpose. They convey irregular surface information where geometry is not available or would not be plausible to do so (for example, the surface texture of a piece of clothing or the scaly skin of a creature). The main differences between the two kinds of maps are the method of creating them and the quality of their results.

Bump maps are created by using a black-and-white image to convey height. White conveys higher; black conveys lower. On the contrary, a normal map is an RGB image that will calculate the vector of the light direction to convey depth much more realistically. Because it is not grayscale, a normal map is not used in the alpha channel of an image.

Displacement Maps Displacement Mapping is fairly new to the game industry. It actually uses the height information conveyed as a black-and-white image to push and pull the pixels of the texture file to adjust the texture perspective according to the camera view. This is pretty neat stuff—but for the purposes of our project, we will not use it. Your Art Director should be able to let you know if Displacement Mapping will be used in your project.

Note: Depending on the game engine and how the graphics are handled, some alpha channel maps can be used as separate texture files instead. Because our Silenus project is being made with only Maya software and no game engine, we need to use most of these alpha channel effects as basic texture maps, rather than alpha channel effects, to see their results.

UV Mapping the Sword

Before we spend too much time on the different texture options that are available (we will get back to them soon) and while the concept of UVs is still fresh in your mind, let's start UV Mapping Silenus. First, we will UV map his sword to get the hang of the process.

One thing to keep in mind when planning your textures is what kind of game you are developing. Obviously, you can expect this 3500-polygon character to be rather prominently featured in the game. The sword may also be very visible. With this information, you can more accurately plan what resolution textures you will want to use. I am going to plan for a texture map that is 256×256 for the sword. For development, we will go one Power of Two larger and create the texture at a resolution of 512×512.

1. Open the finished model you completed in Chapter 2, or open Character_Final.mb from Tutorials/Chapter2/Project_Character/Scenes on the CD. Select the character, and hide it from view (Ctrl+H).

> **Note:** To make working with your model's UVs a little easier, you can use one of Maya's pre-saved panel layouts. In your chosen view panel's menus, navigate to **Panels > Saved Layouts > Persp/UV Texture Editor**. If you would like to edit the layouts (as I did—I reversed the Persp/UV Texture Editor layout to be on opposite sides of the screen), you can change them with **Panels > Saved Layouts > Edit Layouts....**

2. With the UV Texture Editor displayed, select the sword's blade. Use **Edit Polygons > Texture > Planar Mapping** UV projection with the mapping direction set to Z (if your model is oriented differently, you will need to change this to whichever direction you are using).

    With the UVs projected, you can see the result in the UV Texture Editor. Projecting the UVs in this manner will map both sides of the blade from the same direction, effectively causing both sides of the sword to share UV space to maximize the texture usage.

3. Right-click in the UV Texture Editor window, and choose the UVs component type. Move, rotate, and scale the UVs to fit them most efficiently (Figure 3.7).

4. For the faces on the square side of the blade, select the faces and use an Automatic Mapping projection command to separate them from the main UV shell (Figure 3.8).

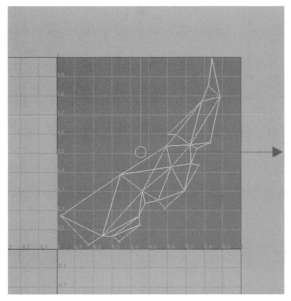

Figure 3.7 Planar map the sword and position the UVs.

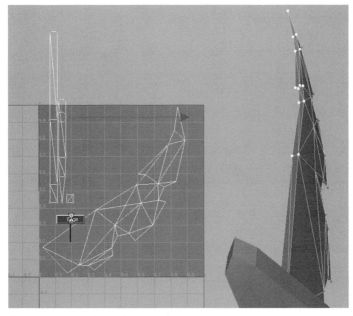

Figure 3.8 Auto map the sword's square edge.

5. In the editor, select the edges that correspond to the edges of the blade. Use the Move and Sew command, and adjust the UVs by hand with the Move Tool to lay out the blade similarly to Figure 3.9.

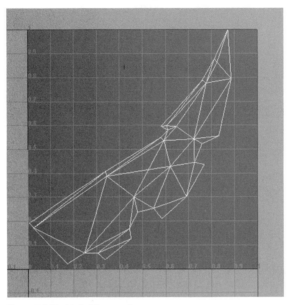

Figure 3.9 The blade UV mapped

Using some sort of grid image on the model to help lay out the UVs is a good idea. This way, you can use the grid to see how your UVs lay on the model and what adjustments need to be made to keep them straight. Navigate on the CD to Images/ `mapping_grid_color.jpg`. You can turn off Show Texture Image in the UV Texture Editor so that you can better see the UVs above the image. (The Hypershade is discussed later in this chapter, if you have trouble applying the image to your model.)

6. Select the faces of the sword grip (excluding the decorative knob on the end), and apply a Cylindrical Mapping projection (Figure 3.10).

7. Scale and position the UV shell, as shown in Figure 3.11.

8. For the tooth-like knob on the end of the grip, use an Automatic Mapping projection. Then use the Move and Sew command and manual tweaking to lay the object's UVs out flat. The tip of the knob can be mapped as a separate piece in the shape of a circle. Scale and position the UVs so that they fit with the sword blade and the rest of the grip (Figure 3.12).

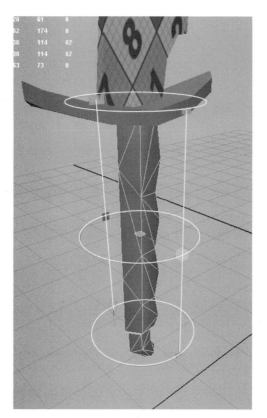

Figure 3.10 Cylindrical map the grip.

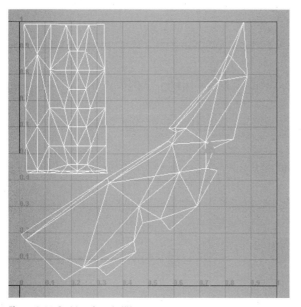

Figure 3.11 Position the grip UVs.

Figure 3.12 UV Mapping the hilt of the grip

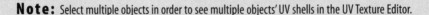

Note: Select multiple objects in order to see multiple objects' UV shells in the UV Texture Editor.

9. For the hand guard of the sword, you can use Automatic Mapping and the Move and Sew command, as well as manual UV positioning, to layout the UVs (Figure 3.13). That finishes the sword.

10. Using UV Snapshot, save the UV layout as an image that can be used as a guide for creating texture in Photoshop (or the 2D editor of your choice). Make it a Targa at 512 × 512 resolution. Save it into either your project directory's images or sourceimages folders.

UV Mapping the Body

Now that the easy sword is UV mapped, it is time to try your new skills at something complicated. Characters are about as complicated as it gets. Because the sword is finished, unhide the character mesh (Shift+Ctrl+H if you are still working in the same session. If not, go to **Display > Show > Show Geometry > Polygon Surfaces**) and hide the sword and the armor. With just the body selected, take a look at the UV Texture Editor (Figure 3.14).

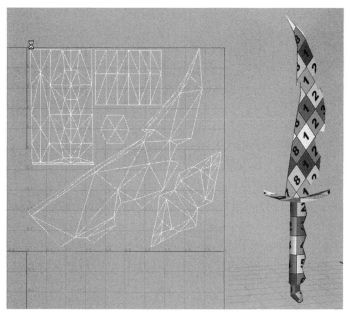

Figure 3.13 Final UV map of the sword

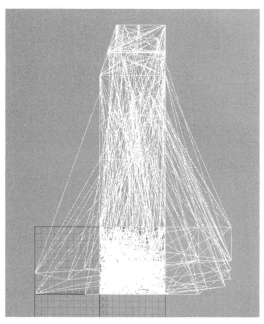

Figure 3.14 The mess of UVs before mapping

Wow! That is quite a mess. (Remember, your results may vary from mine.) So, let's see about cleaning up this mess.

UV Mapping the Torso

We'll first UV map the torso, working our way around the body until the entire model has UVs applied.

1. Detach the head geometry from the body. Select the faces of the head (do not forget the ponytail) and use **Edit Polygons > Extract**. The Extract command will remove the geometry you have selected from the model and turn it into a separate object. Hide it for now.

    If you examine the concept image of Silenus, you can see that his body is very symmetrical. Because the available texture space is limited, we will mirror the texture on one side of the body to the other. Doing so will save a lot of texture space. The easiest way to do this is to actually delete one half of the model, UV map the remaining half, and then duplicate and mirror the geometry. The duplicated geometry will retain the UV coordinates, thereby mirroring the UVs.

2. Delete half of the model's faces. Select the torso geometry, as shown in Figure 3.15.

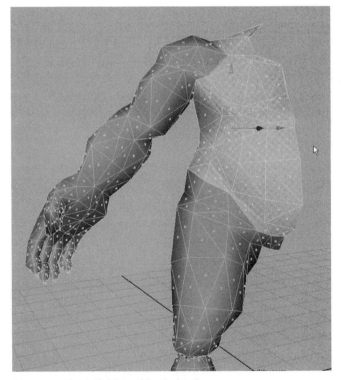

Figure 3.15 Delete half of the model, and select the torso geometry.

3. Use Automatic Mapping to initially lay out the selected geometry's UVs (Figure 3.16). Move these UVs away from the upper-right grid square in the UV Texture Editor to separate them from the rest of the model's UVs. (They are hidden because only our selection is visible.)

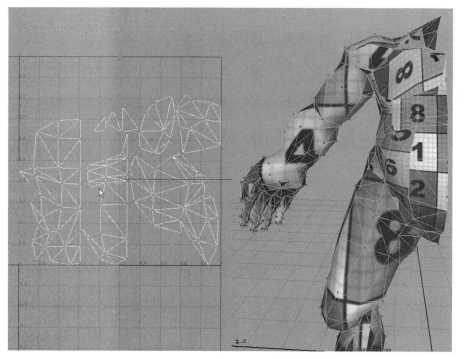

Figure 3.16 Auto Mapping the torso causes multiple UV shells to be laid out across the UV Texture Editor.

4. In the UV Texture Editor, select corresponding edges and use the Move and Sew command to start to piece together the torso UVs. Make sure you deselect edges that correspond to geometry that you do not want to map (for example, that of the legs and arms). (You can apply the colored grid texture to the model if you have not done so.) Once the UVs are sewn together, manually adjust the UVs by hand. Use the grid image as a guide to get the image as straight as possible.

Note: What do I mean when I say "manually adjust the UVs" or "tweak the UVs"? No mapping command or button will produce a perfect UV shell. You will almost always need to manually adjust a UV's position to get the results you need. To do this, use the Move, Rotate, or Scale tools to literally position a UV where you want it. If an edge is sewn somewhere and you want to change it, you will need to select the edge and use the Cut UVs command and then Move and Sew the edge where you need it to go.

There are a couple of ways you can choose to lay out the UVs of the torso. You can have the torso connect at the shoulder or at the side (Figure 3.17). We will sew the UVs at the side because it keeps the UV shell a bit more compact.

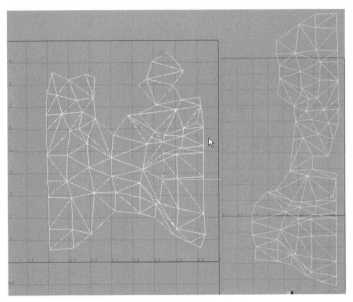

Figure 3.17 Two ways to map the torso: sewn at the side (left) or the shoulder (right)

5.   For now, move the UV shell of the torso to the side, away from the main working area.

UV Mapping the Leg

Next, we will focus on the leg. This is probably the hardest part of UV Mapping the body because of Silenus's rather unconventional leg form. The easiest way to go about this part is to select the major parts of the leg.

1.   Cylindrical map each of the three major sections of the leg. Use the Move and Sew command, and manually tweak the UV positions to get the grid as straight as possible for each section (Figure 3.18).

2.   Use the Move and Sew command, and manually tweak the UVs' positions to attach the different parts together. The trickiest parts are the joints because of the V-joint modeling techniques used (Figure 3.19).

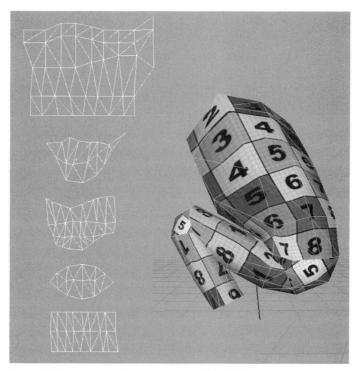

Figure 3.18 Layout of the main sections of the leg in the UV Editor

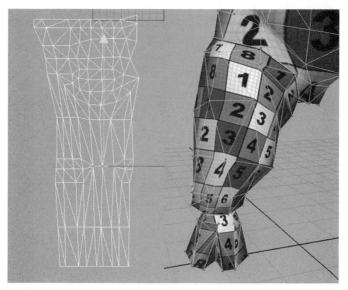

Figure 3.19 Layout of the leg's UVs

Keep in mind where your seam is. The seam of the UV shell is where there is a break in the texture flow on the geometry. You will always want to try to place this seam in as unobtrusive an area as possible. For the leg, you will usually put it along the inner thigh or down the back. For the arms, put it along the underarm, anywhere that would be the least visible during gameplay. The major exception to this is when mirroring UVs across major areas like the chest and head. You will have to rely on your texture painting skills to hide these seams.

3. UV map the hoof separately, as if it were a shoe. To save space, mirror the UVs across the hoof. Select the faces of the hoof, and use an Automatic Mapping projection and manual UV tweaking to straighten out the UVs (Figure 3.20).

Figure 3.20 Beginning the UV layout of the hoof

4. Move the UVs to mirror the UVs across the hoof.

You can mirror the UVs by either of two methods. You can manually move the UVs out from one side of the foot to the other (using Snap to Point to match the UV positions). You can also delete half of the foot, UV map the remaining half, duplicate the remaining half's faces, and mirror the geometry for the other side (Figure 3.21).

5. Planar map (in the Y direction) the bottom of the hoof.

This area of the model will probably not be seen very often, so we can give it a small amount of texture space.

Figure 3.21 The hoof's UVs mirrored

UV Mapping the Arm

The arm is pretty straightforward, as it is primarily cylindrical in shape. However, because of the large muscle formations Silenus has, it is important for the UV layout to be readable for accurate texturing.

1.   Select the faces of the arm, excluding the hand, and apply an Automatic Mapping projection (Figure 3.22).

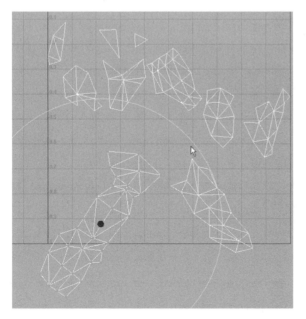

Figure 3.22 The arm after Auto Mapping

2. Move these UVs to the side and use the Move and Sew command, as well as manual tweaking, to straighten out the UVs of the arm. Use the grid texture to help you (Figure 3.23).

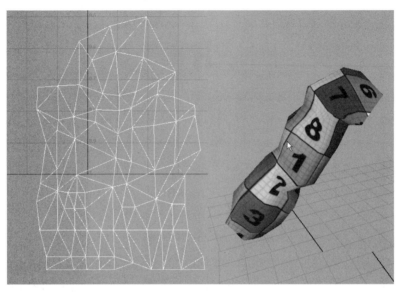

Figure 3.23 Layout of the arm's UVs

The hand is probably even more difficult than our unconventional leg because of the many fingers. Our goal is to use as much texture space as possible as efficiently as possible. With that in mind, we will try to get all four fingers to share the same UV space. To do this, you can delete three of the fingers, UV map one, and then duplicate it for the remaining fingers. You can also manually UV map every finger and match them up by hand. Neither way is easy, and both ways can be time consuming.

3. Select the hand geometry, and apply an Automatic Mapping projection to lay out the geometry you will be using (Figure 3.24).

4. Use the Move and Sew command (along with a lot of tweaking UVs by hand) to lay out the UVs of each finger. Make the layout as clean as possible (Figure 3.25). You can use the Align UVs commands to line UVs together.

5. Stack the fingers on top of each other, using Snap to Point and Align UVs to match applicable points (Figure 3.26). By doing this, you can create one finger texture that will apply to all four.

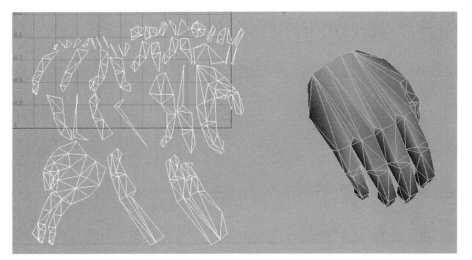

Figure 3.24 Auto Mapping the hand

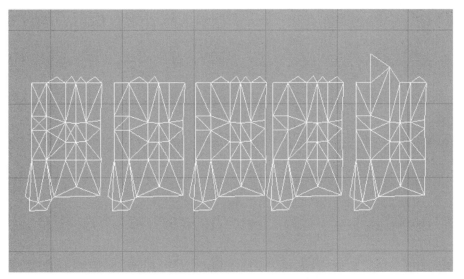

Figure 3.25 Layouts of the four fingers

6. Automatic Map the faces of the thumb to initially lay out the UVs. Then, use the Move and Sew command, along with manual tweaking, to position the UVs (Figure 3.27).

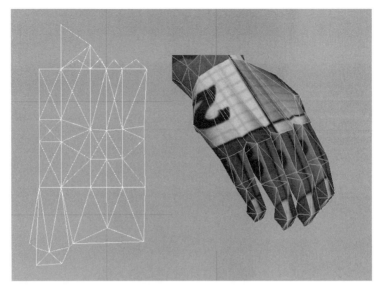

Figure 3.26 The four fingers' UVs stacked on top of each other

Figure 3.27 The thumb UV mapped

7. Planar map the front and back of the palm separately, and then sew them together at one of the sides. (Use the same technique you used to put together the torso.)

The body is now UV mapped. You can duplicate it and mirror it (using the negative scale method or using the Mirror Geometry command under the Polygons menu). Duplicating the half will cause the UVs to be shared on both sides. Attach the two sides together as described in Chapter 2. The next step is to position the UV shells in the upper-right area of the UV Texture Editor for texture preparation (Figure 3.28). You still need to fit the armor on here, so you may need to go back and make some adjustments later.

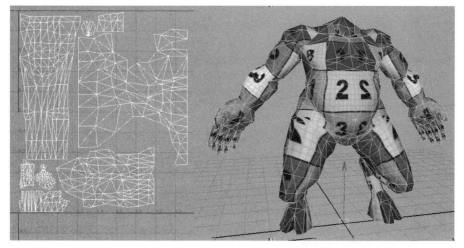

Figure 3.28 The body's UVs mirrored

UV Mapping the Armor

The armor is similar to the body in that we can mirror the UVs for both sides. Therefore, you can delete half of the armor's geometry (the emblem on the chest can remain whole). You probably have noticed a bit of a pattern by now. First, we will lay out the initial UVs by using Automatic Mapping. Then, using editing commands (such as Move and Sew and Align UVs) and manual UV tweaking, you can position the UVs efficiently.

1. For efficient UVs, mirror the shoulder pad UVs not only for the other shoulder, but also for each half of the shoulder pad (Figure 3.29). You can do the same thing for the smaller pad below the main shoulder pad.

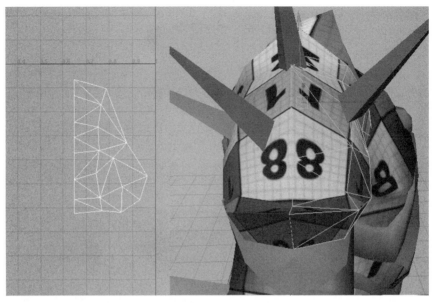

Figure 3.29 Mirroring the UVs of the shoulder pad

2. For the wristband, map the UVs in the same fashion. The faces on the top and bottom of the wristband can share the same UV space (Figure 3.30).

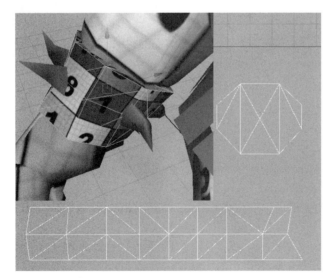

Figure 3.30 The final wristband UV layout

You will want to share UVs for each of the spikes. Let's go over a new command that might help with that. First, lay out the UVs for one of the spikes using the methods that we have already discussed. Now, select the finished spike, shift-select a new spike, and use **Polygons** > **Transfer** (make sure that UV Sets is checked in the Transfer options). This will transfer the UV layout of the first spike to the second. Do this for the rest of the spikes on the wristband. Make sure you delete the spikes' history afterward (**Edit** > **Delete by Type** > **History**). You can repeat the process for the shoulder pad spikes.

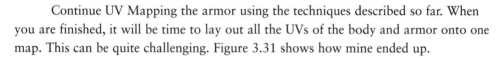

Note: **Polygons** > **Transfer** works only with geometry that is identical in structure. In other words, you cannot transfer UVs from one of the spikes to a totally different object such as Silenus's head.

Continue UV Mapping the armor using the techniques described so far. When you are finished, it will be time to lay out all the UVs of the body and armor onto one map. This can be quite challenging. Figure 3.31 shows how mine ended up.

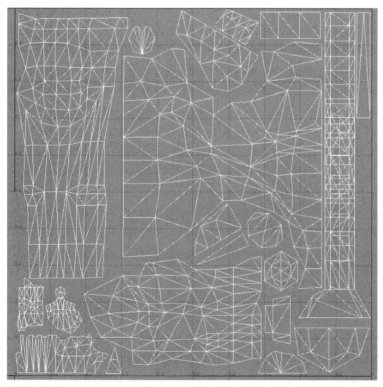

Figure 3.31 Finished UV layout for Silenus's body

UV Layout Tips

Here are some tips and strategies to think about while positioning your UVs:

Sharing UVs Silenus is decked out in a bunch of leather straps. Each of these can obviously be very similar in texture. You can maximize the UV space by overlapping these elements and letting them use the same parts of the texture.

There are a lot of areas where you can maximize UV efficiency by stacking UV shells to share their UV space. The kilt is a prime example. Each slat of the kilt shares UV space. The spikes are another example. Each spike is a three-sided pyramid, so each triangle of an individual spike can be stacked, sharing the UV space.

UV Area Size Applicable to Model Size Small items, such as the spikes on the wristbands and shoulder pads, the jeweled emblem on the chest, etc., should be given applicable texture space. Give a small item a small UV area. On the other side of the coin, large areas, such as the character's torso and legs, should be given as much UV area as possible, because they will be the character's main objects of interest, aside from the head.

One of the major exceptions to this rule is a character's eyes. Eyes are the first things a person looks at, whether it is a game model, an actor, or a person standing next to you. In order to have as much clarity in them as possible, eyes should have a bit more UV area than you would normally think.

Mipmapping *Mipmapping* is the process that the game engine will use to shrink textures by a Power of Two depending on how far the models are from the player's camera view during gameplay. When a model is up close, it will use the maximum size (512×512 in this case). As the player's camera view gets farther and farther from the model, the game engine will automatically switch to a smaller size (256×256, 128×128, etc.). This frees up texture memory that can be given to other objects that are closer to view. Shrinking the texture can cause the pixels to shift very slightly. With that in mind, try to keep at least a little bit of space between UV shells, allowing mipmapping a little leeway when it shrinks textures.

Texture Usage in Gameplay The hair tuft planes on the elbows and back of the legs will be put on the head texture where similar hair from the beard will be mapped. You might do something like this for gameplay. In whatever kind of game Silenus is in, he may use lots of different kinds of armor and costumes. By mapping this hair to the head (which will usually keep the same texture throughout the game), you can avoid having to put this hair in each different armor texture you make.

Use UV Snapshot to create the UV layout as an image you can use in Photoshop. Because you will be planning for a 512 × 512 texture, you will save the layout as a 1024 × 1024, one Power of Two larger.

UV Mapping the Head

For UV Mapping the head, you can again delete half of the model in order to mirror the UVs. You can leave the ponytail whole. However, if you need the UV space later, you can mirror it as well.

Using the Average Vertices command (**Polygons > Average Vertices**) is a new technique you can use. Duplicate the head geometry, and move it to the side. Perform the Average Vertices command, and you should see the vertices shift. This command will make the head's different forms not quite as oblique. You can UV map this less distinct head and transfer the UVs to the original (Figure 3.32).

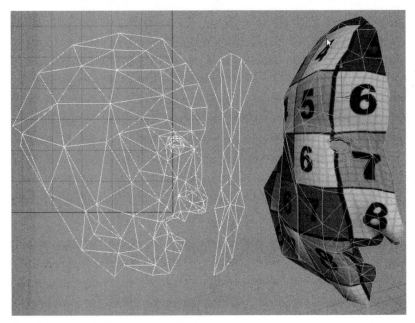

Figure 3.32 Using a duplicate with averaged vertices

Another method is to apply an Automatic Mapping projection to the head, and then apply a Planar Mapping projection to the front of the face (Figure 3.33). You can then use the Move and Sew command and manually UV tweak to connect the main part of the head to the face. This method is probably the better way because it can result in an easier-to-work-with UV layout. It does have some drawbacks in that you will need to meticulously tweak the UVs of the nose and eyes to make sure they do not overlap or stretch. Even so, you will probably see some stretching, but try to minimize it as much as possible.

1. Select the faces of the interior of the mouth and apply an Automatic Mapping projection. Mirror the UVs on the top and bottom of the mouth to save UV space and avoid having to somehow fit the mouth UVs with the rest of the face.

2. Continue UV Mapping the head elements. Duplicate and mirror the halved geometry when you finish. Figure 3.34 shows the finished product.

3. Using UV Snapshot, save a 512×512 image. The final image will be 256×256 when you are finished.

In Figure 3.35, you can see the finished UV mapped model.

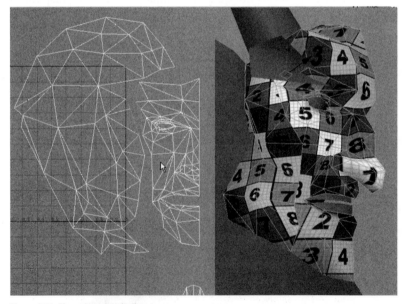

Figure 3.33 Planar Mapping the face

Figure 3.34 The finished head UV layout

Figure 3.35 The completed UV-mapped character

The Hypershade

They Hypershade window is Maya's primary editor for creating materials and textures for your models. You can navigate to this window by going to **Window > Rendering Editors > Hypershade**. The Hypershade is capable of creating quite a large variety of very complex materials. For game development, however, our needs for the Hypershade are not nearly that demanding.

Maya comes with a variety of *materials*. A material can be described as a representation of the general surface properties of an object: how shiny it is, how glossy it is, how luminescent it is, etc. Texture files can be applied to a material's different attributes to control these factors to an exact degree. There are any number of ways that a game engine can use textures and materials. Sometimes, all you have to do is apply your main color texture, and the game engine will apply any other maps (bump map, spec map, etc.) automatically by referencing the file name. Other times, you may need to apply the maps to particular material attributes for it to work. Your Art Director should be able to let you know how you need to handle material usage at a job.

However, because we are working totally in Maya, we will do things very traditionally. We will apply the bump map to the bump attribute and the transparency map to the transparency attribute.

Applying a Material to a Model

On the left side of the Hypershade is the Create Bar. It lists the available materials, *procedural textures* (textures provided by Maya), etc.

1. Left-click on a Lambert material in the list. A new Lambert material will appear in the large window on the right. Click this button two more times, creating three Lambert materials.

A *Lambert* material is a material without any specularity. If you decide to change this material later, you can change it in the Attribute Editor (Ctrl+A while it is selected).

2. Rename these materials to Head, Body, and Sword.

 Note: There are many ways to rename a material. The easiest way is to double-click on each material and enter a new name at the top of the Attribute Editor that opens.

Now you want to apply these new materials to the geometry that will correspond to the three textures you will create for the sword, the body, and the head.

3. Select all the objects that will have a single material applied, right-click on the material in the Hypershade, and choose Assign Material to Selection from the marking menu that appears. Do this for each material.

Do not forget that you will apply the hair planes on the legs to the head material.

Applying a Texture to a Material

Once you have a material, you can begin to apply texture maps to the material's different attributes. The most obvious attribute to map is Color. This will control the brunt of what you actually see on the model. To apply a texture to the color attribute, open the material's Attribute Editor (Ctrl+A or double-click the material in the Hypershade). Next to the Color attribute (and most of the other attributes) is a small button with a black-and-white checker pattern. This is the Mapping button. Clicking it will open the Create Render Node window where you can choose what kind of texture you will apply to the attribute.

In most game art, you will want to choose a File texture. This will let you apply custom textures that you create in Photoshop (or another 2D application) to your model, rather than a procedural texture that comes with Maya.

1. After choosing File from the window, click the browse button (a folder icon) next to the Image Name text box in the File's attributes. This browse button will allow you to navigate through your directories and choose the texture file you want to use.

2. In your view panel, make sure Hardware Texturing is turned on under the panel's shading menu, or press the **6** key in order to view the textures in your scene.

> **Note:** To remove a texture from a material's mapped attributes, right-click on the attribute and choose Break Connection from the popup menu.

Optional Procedures

The following procedures are not necessary for creating a model, but they can either help the process or enhance the model's visuals. The 3D Paint Tool is very helpful for creating texture guides. Vertex Coloring can add color variations to a model without changing a texture, or add lighting information. *Baking normal maps* is a process that generates a normal map pixel shader. Obviously, make sure your game supports normal maps before taking the time to make one.

> **Note:** PSD texture support is new to Maya 6. Instead of choosing a File texture, choose PSD so you can use your Photoshop file for your work in progress. Final textures, however, generally tend to be in `.tga` or `.tif` formats.

Game Artist: John Paul Sommer

Job Title Art Director

Studio Warthog Texas

Credits *Freelancer, Motocross Madness, Deadly Tide, Ravage, Starlancer, Conquest: Frontier Wars, Conquest 2: Vyrium Uprising, Fallen Kingdoms*

Studio Site www.warthogtx.com

Personal Site www.S3DA.com

Q. How and why did you get into the game industry?

A. My introduction into the game industry began with a small developer located in Phoenix, AZ. I soon realized that I really enjoyed the allowance of creativity. Although I was fully up to speed in animation, I was not hired because I was the best animator, but simply because of my passion for the industry, which reflected throughout my work. I got the job simply because I loved doing it, and I chose the game industry as a career because I truly love art and animation. Fantasy and Science Fiction has always fascinated me and by developing games, this gives me the opportunity to create environments and characters that reflect that fascination. I cannot imagine anything better than creating a character, animating it, and ultimately using it to wreak havoc on a fully detailed 3D world.

Q. Describe your role at your studio.

A. My role as Art Director requires me to manage a team of artists, deal with schedules, and develop the overall look and feel of the game. I am ultimately responsible for everything visual that goes into the game, from the GUI (Graphic User Interface) to the FMV (Full Motion Video).

Q. What has been the most inspirational to you in regard to your artwork?

A. This is a tough question, being that there are so many things that I draw inspiration from. I draw a lot of my inspiration from my fellow artists and peers. Other sources include: photography, sculpture, painters (both traditional and digital), movies, and the thousands of talented artists that are on the Internet.

Q. What is your favorite artistic style?

A. My style changes all the time, I love to experiment and learn new styles. One day, it might be photo-realism, the next it may be abstract photography, or perhaps even Impressionism. I think every style has something about it that inspires me to continue learning in every facet possible.

Continues on next page

Game Artist: John Paul Sommer *(continued)*

Q. What is your favorite kind of game?

A. First Person Shooters! First Person Shooters allows the players to actually immerse them-selves not only into the game but also into the feel of the game. They really put you in the middle of all the action.

Q. How do you use Maya in your specific job?

A. I mostly use Maya for the full-motion video and animation. However, overall I use Maya for all facets of game development, from concept to final production. I have learned that it is a great tool to experiment with as well as visualizing the general look and feel of any project.

Q. What about Maya do you like better than other 3D apps?

A. I like how interactive Maya is. It is an exceptional tool. The biggest advantage Maya has over other 3D apps is the User Interface (UI). I have used just about every 3D app on the shelf, and Maya's UI is simply the best and most intuitive. Another advantage of Maya versus other pro-grams is the fact that it does not require a ton of plug-ins to get the job done. Everything you need to get your job done quickly and easily is right at your fingertips.

Q. Which Maya tool could you not live without?

A. Set Driven Key! This is one of the most powerful features in Maya. It can make animation so much more enjoyable with just a little bit of setup time. There are really many tools I could not live without, but this single feature is at the top of the list.

Q. What advice might you have for the up-and-coming game artist?

A. My advice would simply be to work hard in everything you do. You should always work toward self-improvement. Make sure you are well prepared to accomplish your tasks, and of course…*practice, practice, practice!* The most important piece of advice I can give the new game artist is this: Your portfolio may get you in the door, but a great attitude will keep you there! Having a positive "can do" and "will do" attitude is invaluable in this industry. Mix that in with a lot of creativity and you are set!

The 3D Paint Tool

When you are texturing a model, creating a guide to the major parts of the body for the UV layout can be very helpful. A guide can spare you a lot of grief if you have trouble recognizing the various parts of the model within the jumble of lines that make up UV layouts. The 3D Paint Tool can help you accomplish this, but it can be a little confusing if you are not familiar with it.

First of all, the model has to be UV mapped, and it needs to have a material applied (without a color map) for the 3D Paint Tool to work properly. When these two criteria are met, you can get started.

To avoid confusion, hide everything except the objects to which your current material is applied. Start with the sword, so you can hide the body and the head. Here are the steps:

1. Combine the three sections of the sword together into one. With the sword selected, go to the Rendering module (F5) and go to **Texturing** > **3D Paint Tool** > **Options.**

2. Scroll down in the 3D Paint Tool options toward the bottom. Under the File Textures section, choose the Image Format (I chose Targa) and click the Assign/Edit Textures button. A small window will pop up; you can use it to enter how large the image will be. For the sword, choose a 512 × 512 image to match your UV layout. This enables the brush.

3. To resize your brush, manipulate the radius attributes at the top of the Paint Tool options. You can also hold the B key and click and drag with the middle or left mouse button. Paint on the model to mark it up and help you in the texture painting process.

   Don't try to be too perfect, as this is mainly a guide and usually should not be incorporated into the texture itself. Once you have the model marked up a bit to indicate where the major parts are in the UV layout, you will need to save it.

4. In the File Textures section of the Paint Tool options, click the Save Textures button. This will save the texture file into the 3DPaintTextures folder of your project directory.

Continue with the body and the head, following the same steps. Remember to combine the geometry together to help make the painting easier. You can later use **Edit Polygons** > **Separate** to undo this. My results are shown in Figure 3.36.

Vertex Coloring

Vertex coloring is one method that some game engines use to add large swaths of color to a model without having to edit the texture files. Many game engines project lighting onto models using vertex coloring as well. To apply per-vertex coloring in Maya, select the geometry, and navigate to **Edit Polygons** > **Colors** > **Paint Vertex Color Tool** > **Options.** This tool works very similarly to the 3D Paint Tool, and it uses a brush to paint on color. You can change the color in the options, under the Color section.

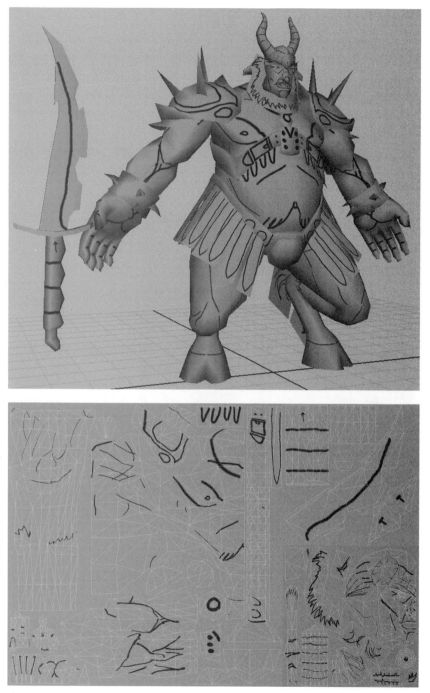

Figure 3.36 A texture guide created with the 3D Paint tool

Baking Normal Maps

A *normal map*, as described earlier, is a pixel shader that uses light information to calculate very accurate bump mapping in real time. The image is RGB, with the three hues controlling XYZ depth, respectively. One method for creating a normal map is to actually create a high-resolution version of the model in addition to the low-polygon version and baking that information down into a normal map using Maya 6's new Transfer Surface Information function.

First, you need to create a high polygon version of your game model. Also, your low-polygon model must be UV mapped. For this example, we will use Silenus's horn (Figure 3.37).

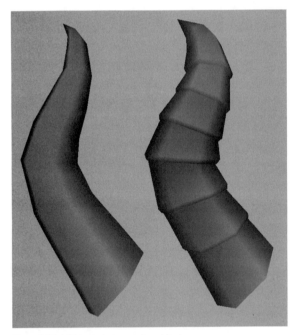

Figure 3.37 A high-resolution version of the horn

1. Place the high-resolution model over the low-resolution model.
2. Select the low-poly model first and shift-select the high-poly model.
3. Under the Rendering module, go to **Lighting/Shading > Transfer Surface Information > Options**.

Note: Make sure the plug-in, `TransferSurfaceInfo.ml1`, is loaded under **Window > Settings/Preferences > Plug-In Manager**.

In the options, you can set the image resolution, file location and name, and file format. You may need to experiment with the Search Depth when making your normal maps. Search Depth indicates how far from the low-poly model it needs to look to properly calculate the normal map.

4. When ready, click the Bake button and Maya will calculate the normal map and save it to the indicated location.

Texture Painting Tips

Texture painting is definitely a process that depends a lot on talent and practice. Here are some tips to keep in mind while painting your own textures.

Contrast Make sure that your texture is not too subtle. Folds, wrinkles, etc. need to be very clear to be conveyed in the texture. Making sure the image has some contrast can help with this.

Hand Painting versus Photo Sourcing There are two main schools of thought when it comes to creating textures: paint them by hand or use photo sources. Personally, I do both. But even when I use photos of some kind, I rarely use them as is, and I will always try to customize what I take from photos.

The method you use will generally be determined by the style of the game. A game like *The Legend of Zelda: The Wind Waker* probably would not use much in the way of photo sourcing because of the cartoon style.

Note: A great source for high-resolution photo references is www.3d.sk.

Saturation Color saturation can depend a lot on the style of the game, but you want to make sure that the nice pretty colors you choose in Photoshop show up nicely on the model.

The Finished Model

For the final Silenus model, we have the following textures:

Color Maps The color maps are the main textures that you see with all of the color information (Figure 3.38). These images are mapped to the Color attribute of your materials.

Specular Maps The specular maps are grayscale images with specularity information. Wherever the model should be shiny, the texture should be white (Figure 3.39). If you use specular maps, you will need to change your Lambert material into one that is capable of specularity, such as a blinn. This is easily done in the material's Attribute Editor by changing the Type attribute near the top.

Specular maps are mapped to the Specular Color attribute of your materials.

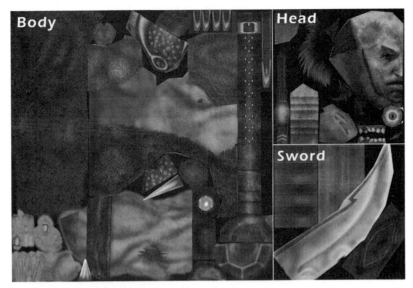

Figure 3.38 The three color maps for Silenus

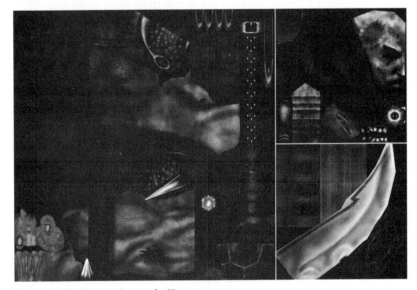

Figure 3.39 The three specular maps for Silenus

Transparency Maps As mentioned before, transparency maps (or opacity maps) will make a model transparent where the texture is black. White areas will remain opaque (Figure 3.40). Transparency maps are mapped to the Transparency attribute of your materials.

 Note: Maya will automatically apply the alpha channel of your color maps to the Transparency attribute.

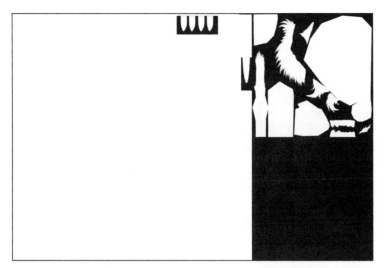

Figure 3.40 The two transparency maps for Silenus

Bump Maps As technology has increased, bump maps have rapidly become replaced with normal maps. But essentially, white areas indicate high, while black areas indicate low. Bump maps are mapped to the Bump Mapping attribute of your materials.

Because this book is not in color, I will not show the bump maps here. Essentially, they are grayscale versions of the color maps. All of the maps I used can be found on the CD under `Tutorials/Chapter3/Character_UVMapping/sourceimages`.

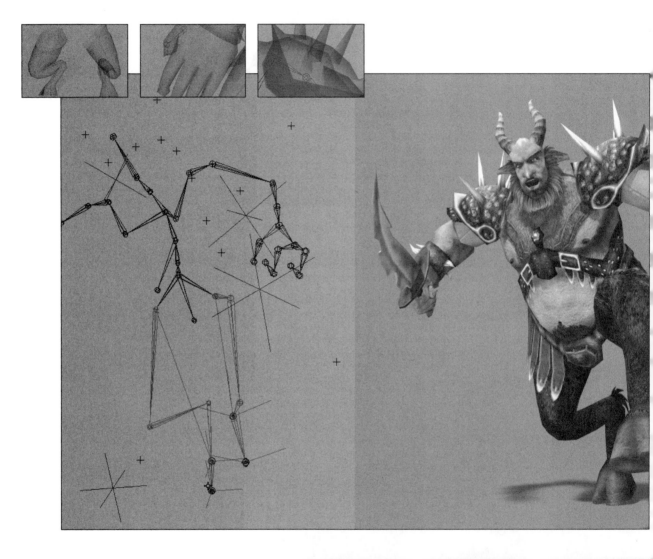

Rigging

Silenus looks good, but he will not last long in battle if he cannot move. Rigging *is the process of setting up the controls on a model to allow it to move and be animated. In most cases, you use a* skeleton *to set up a rig. A skeleton is comprised of a hierarchy of* joints *(or bones) that you consciously disperse throughout the body. They act as a structure on which animation can take place. In this chapter, you will learn how to create a skeleton for games, and you'll learn about other useful rigging techniques and concepts.*

Chapter Contents

Skeletons and Joints

A skeleton composed of joints is the main rigging component of any *deforming* (bending) model. For games, the number of joints in your skeleton is very important. A joint threshold will limit the number of joints your skeletons can have, much the same as polycounts limit the number of polygons you can have. The joint threshold varies greatly from game to game, and it is usually based on the number of characters your game simultaneously features on the screen. A real-time strategy (RTS) game, with its armies of swarming characters, requires fewer joints per unit than a fighting game with only two combatants on the screen. As the technological advancements in the game industry have grown, this threshold increases. Make sure your project manager lets you know what kind of limitations your game has in a real job.

You can form a game character's skeleton very similar to that of a real skeleton. Rather than muscle and sinew, you *bind* your geometry to the joints which attaches the individual vertices to the closest joints. You can then adjust the amount of *weight* or influence that each joint has on the vertices to control the amount of deformation each joint has.

Let's take this one step at a time, though. The process of placing your individual joints is critical because making changes can be very difficult after you have bound and adjusted the weights.

Creating a Skeleton

All rigging tools and commands are under the Animation module. You'll use the Joint tool to create the skeleton. Because this tool depends on precise placement, I recommend using the orthographic views (side, front, top) when you place joints in your scene.

Although the number of joints in a real game can be limited, you can use as many joints as you want or need to in this example. As you improve, you will learn how to use fewer joints when necessary. Try to be efficient, however, and don't place joints indiscriminately.

The Pelvis and Legs

The first joint of your skeleton is known as the skeleton's *root joint*. This is the joint that will control the entire skeleton as a whole. For most creatures, whether human or otherwise, the root joint is the pelvis.

1.   Open your completed model (or copy the `Tutorials/Chapter4/Character_Rigging` directory to your hard drive and open the `Rigging_Start.mb` file from the directory's Scenes folder).

2.   Go to **Skeleton > Joint Tool**. In the front view, hold the X key to grid snap and snap a joint to the center grid line in the middle of the character. This is the root joint, which will be the pelvis of the skeleton.

3. While still in the front view, release the X key and place another joint about one unit to the character's left and one unit down. This will act as a hip joint for Silenus's left leg.

4. Click once more to place another joint at the approximate location of the knee, about 2.5 units down and 1.5 units to the character's left.

5. Switch to the side view. Click and drag with the middle mouse button to reposition the most recent joint to better fit the knee at this angle.

6. While still in the side view, place a new joint at Silenus's "second knee." This is effectively the ankle.

7. Place another joint at the top of the hoof, and place a last joint down to the floor line.

If you return to the front view, you will see that the new joints, while they look fine in the side view, are obviously off in the front view. Press the Enter key to exit out of the Joint tool, and press the Insert key to enter pivot mode. Pivot mode allows you to change an object's pivot point; however, it also lets you reposition a joint without affecting the rest of the joints in the chain. Using this mode, you can reposition the ankle and two hoof joints to fit the front view's perspective. At this point, you should have something similar to Figure 4.1.

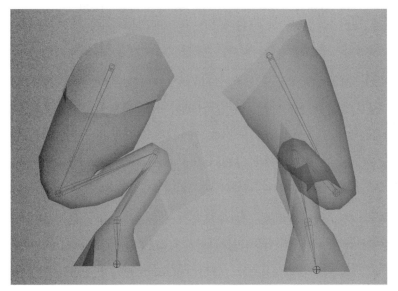

Figure 4.1 The leg joints in place

If two joints are not linked properly (for example, if the hip joint is not linked to the pelvis joint), you can connect them by first selecting the hip joint and then Shift+select the pelvis joint. Then press the P hotkey to *parent* the hip to the pelvis (or **Edit > Parent**). This will create the connection between the two joints. This connection is in a *hierarchy* (or "chain of command," if you will). The parent object is at the top, while the *children* are below. Wherever the parent goes, the children follow. In the case of skeletons, you are creating a chain of joint hierarchies—one joint parented to the next, which is in turn parented to the next, etc.

Go ahead and rename the joints. If you followed along with this example, rename them as follows:

joint1	Pelvis
joint2	L_Hip
joint3	L_Knee
joint4	L_Ankle
joint5	L_Hoof1
joint6	L_Hoof2

8. To accurately mirror the leg joints to the other side, select L_Hip and go to **Skeleton > Mirror Joint > Options**. In the options, select the direction to mirror. (In this example, the direction is YZ.) In the Replacement Names for Duplicated Joints section, input the following:

   Search For: L

   Replace With: R

   Both legs should now be prefixed with L and R for the left and right legs, respectively.

The Spine

The spine will be a series of evenly spaced joints that run up the curvature of the character's back.

1. In the side view, using the Joint tool, place the first joint very close to the pelvis joint, about .25 units up and behind.

   The first joint is so close to the pelvis because the pelvis joint itself will control the orientation of the entire skeleton. If you want the character to bend at the waist, you will need this new joint so that it can.

2. Continue along the back of the character. Place about three more joints, and end about even with the shoulders (Figure 4.2).

3. Starting at the base of the spine and moving toward the neck, rename these joints Back1, Back2, Back3, and Back4.

4. Place a new joint at the base of the neck, and place a second through the character's forehead in front of the face. To complete the spine, parent the neck joint to Back4.

5. Rename these joints as Neck and Head (Figure 4.3).

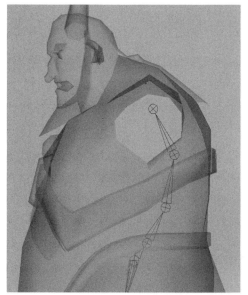

Figure 4.2 The spine joints along the back of the character

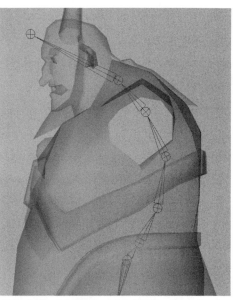

Figure 4.3 The joints of the neck and head complete the spine.

The Arms

The arms are a bit more complicated than you might think. Rather than just the shoulder, elbow, and wrist that you find in a real arm, you will need to place a few extra joints for the forearm, shoulder, and where the arm meets the spine. These extra joints will help give the character a sturdy framework and the ability to deform properly.

1. In the front view, start the arm by placing a joint at about the character's middle-left chest. Continue up into the shoulder and place two joints, as seen in Figure 4.4.

The first shoulder joint will help keep the shoulder's deformation clean when bending, and it will act as an anchor for the shoulder pad. The second joint will be the actual shoulder pivot for the arm.

2. From here, place a joint at the elbow, another one halfway between the elbow and wrist for the forearm, and a last one for the wrist itself (Figure 4.5).

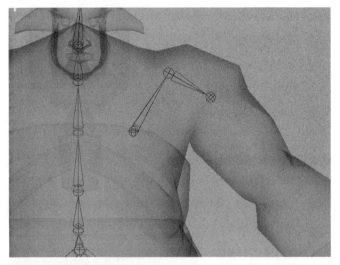

Figure 4.4 The joints of the shoulder

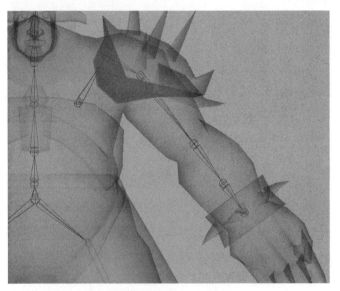

Figure 4.5 The arm joints in place

3. Parent the chest joint to the center back joint to connect it to the hierarchy.

4. Switch to the perspective view, and make sure the entire arm chain is in place within the geometry. Starting from the chest and working your way to the wrist, rename the joints as follows:

L_Chest

L_ShoulderPad

L_Shoulder

L_Elbow

L_Forearm

L_Wrist

5. Rotate the L_Shoulder joint so that the elbow joint is back toward the elbow of the geometry. Rotate the L_Elbow joint to position the L_Wrist joint in the center of the geometry at the wrist.

The reason you rotate the joints is to give the skeleton a natural bend at the elbow. You will also want to do this in the knees when you are working with a more human-style character.

The Hands

The hands of a game skeleton can be constructed a number of ways, depending on the gameplay and the kind of movements that the game needs. A shooting game, for example, may require only the thumb and index finger to have any range of movement. This example will use this common method.

Because of the angle of the hand, no orthographic view will really let you place joints correctly, so you will need to place the joints in the scene and then move them into place.

1. In the front view, place a two-joint chain over where the thumb is. In the perspective view, move them on the hand as in Figure 4.6.

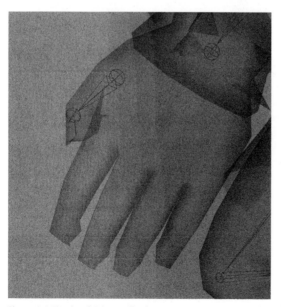

Figure 4.6 The thumb joints set in place

2. Back in the front view, place a three-joint chain in the scene over the fingers and position them in the perspective view on the index finger.

3. Using the same technique, duplicate the chain (Ctrl+D), and place it on the ring finger.

4. Create a single joint, and place it in the palm toward the pinky finger.

5. Parent the different joints as follows:

   a. Parent the palm joint to the wrist.

   b. Parent the two fingers' joint chains to the palm joint.

   c. Parent the thumb-joint chain to the wrist.

   You should have something similar to Figure 4.7.

6. Using an L prefix to designate "left," name your joints.

7. Mirror the joints of the arm by selecting the L_Chest joint and using **Skeleton > Mirror Joint**. (Make sure the Find and Replace settings are set to change the L prefix to R.)

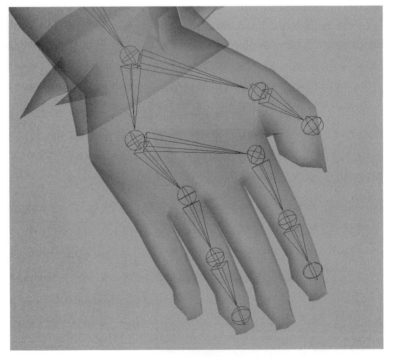

Figure 4.7 The finished hand joints

Extra Joints

Depending on how many joints you are budgeted, you may not have room for extra joints. Extra joints help keep the shape of the model together at high-stress points (such as the groin or, as in this example, the abdomen). Joints such as these aren't absolutely necessary, but they can make the process of distributing the skeleton's weight over the geometry easier.

1. In the side view, place a joint in the center of the belly, and parent it to one of the middle-back joints.

2. Place another joint below the pelvis in the groin area, and parent it to the pelvis. Your finished skeleton should look similar to Figure 4.8.

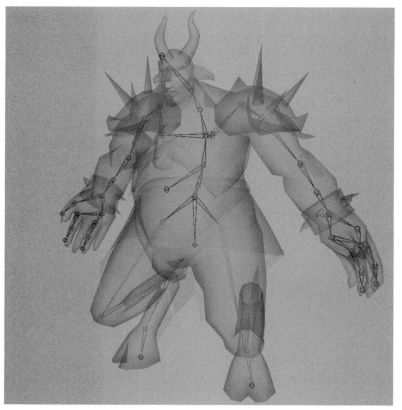

Figure 4.8 The completed skeleton

Setting the Local Rotation Axis

The rotation of objects and joints alike can be set to Global (aligned with the scene) or Local (aligned with itself) rotation. To make animation easier, make sure the Local Rotation Axis of each joint is aligned with the direction of its bone.

Note: To switch between Global and Local rotation, access the options by double-clicking the Rotate tool or Left-click+E to access a quick-select radial menu.

1. Select the pelvis joint, and use **Skeleton > Orient Joint**.

   This will align each joint along whichever axis is set in the command's options. For now, just use the default option of XYZ. This does not always work perfectly, and you will most likely need to adjust the local rotation axis of some joints manually. In this case, the fingers, chest, and pelvis joints are the most blatant that need to be fixed.

2. Select one of the finger joints, and toggle the Select by Component Type mode in the Status line (F8).

   This switches you to component mode. The component selection masks are to the right of the toggled button.

3. On the far right of the available masks, select the button indicated by a question mark (?) labeled "Select by Component Type: Miscellaneous."

4. For the selected joint (as well as those below it in the hierarchy), a small axis symbol appears. Select this, and rotate it to align with the direction of the bone (Figure 4.9). Repeat this procedure for any joint that is not aligned along the bone.

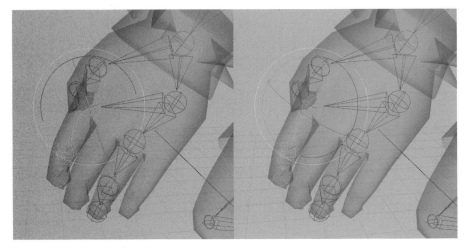

Figure 4.9 Changing the local rotation axis

Forward and Inverse Kinematics

Forward Kinematics (FK) and Inverse Kinematics (IK) are two manipulation techniques used in animation to control the bending of joints in a chain. Forward Kinematics is the method of rotating joints in order *down* the hierarchy. For example, we will use FK for the arms. When animating them, we will rotate each joint individually from shoulder, to elbow, to wrist, etc.

Inverse Kinematics is what we will use for the legs. This way, we can select the foot and moving it will automatically affect the knee and hip *up* the hierarchy.

Leg IK

To use Inverse Kinematics, you have to create an IK handle between the joints that you want to animate. In this example, you'll create a handle for the legs.

1. Go to **Skeleton > IK Handle Tool > Options**. In the options, set Current Solver to ikRPsolver and check the Sticky option. Close the Options window.

    Turning on the Sticky option will make the feet "stick" to their position. This will make it easier to keep Silenus's feet even with the floor plane while he is walking and running.

> **Note:** The ikRPsolver adds Rotate Plane attributes that allow us to create a control for knee orientation in the next section.

2. With the IK Handle tool active, click once on the L_Hip and then click the L_Hoof1 joints.

    An IK handle will be created between the two selected joints. You can test this by moving the handle created at the hoof. The L_Knee and L_Ankle joints should bend realistically (Figure 4.10).

3. Repeat the process with the right leg.

Adding Knee Controls

You need to add a control for the knee's orientation. The easiest way to do this is by creating a *locator*. Think of locators as empty objects that can be used in a variety of ways (such as constraint targets, handles, or custom attribute controllers). In this example, we will use them as constraint targets and handles for the knee controls.

1. Go to **Create > Locator**.
2. Move this new object in front of the left knee.

3. Select the locator, and Shift+select the IK handle (in that order). Go to **Constrain > Pole Vector.**

This creates a Pole Vector constraint between the IK handle and the locator.

When you move the locator now, the knee will remain pointed in the locator's direction (Figure 4.11).

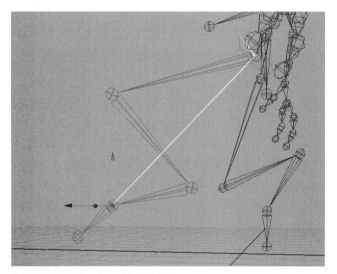

Figure 4.10 An IK handle used in the left leg

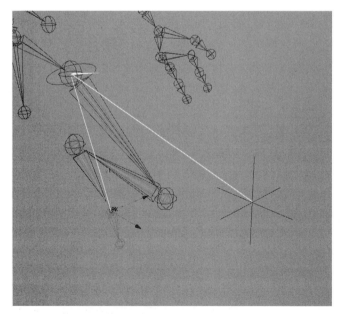

Figure 4.11 The knee controls in place

4. Repeat the process with the right leg.

Note: If joints shift out of place after constraining the IK handles to the locators, move the locators to fit the joints back into the geometry.

Rename the IK handles L_LegIK and R_LegIK, respectively. Rename the locators L_Knee_Locator and R_Knee_Locator.

Foot IK

To control the angle of the foot (or hoof, in this case), you need to create a new IK handle.

1. With the IK Handle tool, click first on the L_Hoof1 joint and then on the L_Hoof2 joint. This creates a small IK handle between the two joints of the hoof (Figure 4.12).

2. Repeat the process with the right hoof.

3. Rename the IK handles to L_FootIK and R_FootIK.

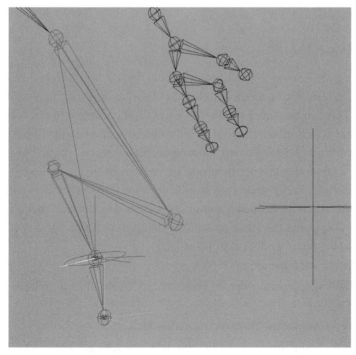

Figure 4.12 The foot IK in place

Adding Foot Controls

To add foot controls:

1. Select the L_FootIK and group it (Ctrl+G or **Edit > Group**) to itself.

2. Press the Insert key to enter pivot mode, and point snap (V) the pivot of the group to the L_Hoof2 joint. Rename this group L_Toe. Press Insert again to exit pivot mode.
    You can use this group to orient the direction of the hoof.

3. Select both the L_LegIK and the L_Toe group. Group the two together.

4. Press the Insert key to enter pivot mode and point snap (V) the pivot of the group to the L_Hoof1 joint. Press Insert again to exit pivot mode.

    By grouping the two IK handles together, you now have a single control for both the leg movement and the foot angle.

5. Repeat the process for the right foot.

6. Rename the groups L_Foot and R_Foot.

7. Parent the knee locators to their respective foot groups.

    Parenting the locators to the foot will keep the knee pointing forward during movement without having to keep manually moving the locators to follow the character around as he animates.

Displaying Selection Handles

With the IK handles and skeleton in place, you can now display selection handles for the major points of movement. Selection handles allow you to easily access the skeleton over the geometry. This can be done a number of ways. You could create elaborate curve objects to act as selection handles, but I tend to use the simpler selection handles that can be displayed through Maya's own functions. Creating curve objects for your skeleton controls is a good idea if more than one animator is using the skeleton, because you can illustrate exactly what each handle does for those unfamiliar with your setup. This does take time, however, and under a strict deadline you may not have that kind of luxury. Displaying the selection handles that are native to Maya, while not as descriptive, is simpler, faster, and works just as well.

To display the selection handles:

1. Select the following joints in order: L_ShoulderPad, L_Shoulder, L_Elbow, and L_Wrist.

2. Go to **Display > Component Display > Selection Handles**.

    Small crosshairs should appear in the locations of the selected joints. These crosshairs are not useful in their current positions, though. You need to move them outside the geometry.

3. Toggle the Select by Component Type button in the Status line (F8). In the available component selection masks, choose the Select by Component Type: Handles button indicated by a crosshair. Make certain no other selection mask is active.

4. Select and move the selection handles of the indicated joints outside of the geometry. This will make them easy to access.

5. Repeat for the right arm.

   Repeat this process for the four back joints, neck joint, pelvis joint, and the two foot groups (Figure 4.13).

6. To create a selection handle for moving the entire character, select the pelvis joint and both foot groups and group them (Ctrl+G). Display the group's selection handle and place it within easy access. Rename the group Silenus.

Figure 4.13 The displayed skeleton selection handles

Armor Parenting

Not every object on the character will be bound to the skeleton on a per-vertex basis. Nondeforming parts, such as the shoulder pads and hair planes, can be parented to the skeleton. This will cause them to move with the skeleton without deforming.

1. Select the spikes and small pad on the left shoulder, and then Shift+select the main shoulder pad. Press the P key to parent the smaller objects to the main shoulder pad.

2. Select the main shoulder pad, Shift+select the L_ShoulderPad joint. Parent the shoulder pad to the selected joint.

By using the two shoulder joints, you can accurately animate the *secondary motion* of the shoulder pads while the arm moves. Secondary motion is motion that is a direct result of the primary motion. For example, while Silenus runs, the shoulder pads will bounce slightly.

Using the same procedures you used with the shoulders, perform the following steps:

1. Parent the wristband spikes to the wrist joint.

2. Parent the leg-hair planes to the ankle joint.

3. Parent the arm-hair plane to the elbow joint.

4. Parent the chest jewel to the Back4 joint.

Binding to the Skeleton

Now that the skeleton is complete, you can bind it to the geometry. Two types of binding are available: *smooth binding* and *rigid binding*. Smooth binding allows each vertex to be affected by more than one joint. This type of binding tends to result in a smoother transition during animation. Rigid binding restricts each vertex so that it is only affected by a single joint. Although some tools allow a rigid-bound skeleton to bend more smoothly, rigid binding is usually used to lock nondeformable objects to certain joints. Parenting (as you did earlier) produces the same results, so you will be using smooth binding for the character.

Don't bind the head yet. Just hide it for now. You can also hide all of the parented geometry: the shoulder pads, hair planes, wristband spikes, etc. When you are done, only the geometry that will be bound to the skeleton and not parented in some way should be left (Figure 4.14).

Before you continue, make sure that the geometry is complete. Extensively adjusting the geometry after binding can be a hassle. At this point, you should select all the geometry and delete the *History* (**Edit > Delete by Type > History**). The History keeps track of all of the changes you have made over the course of the project, and

Figure 4.14 The geometry to be bound

keeping this information consumes memory. Binding the geometry to the skeleton, however, applies important History to the scene that must remain for the binding to function correctly. You cannot partially delete History, so go ahead and delete any History your geometry has before you bind the skeleton. Doing so bakes all previous editing into the model, giving you a clean slate before binding takes place.

Note: History in Maya, while also a running record of a user's actions, is mainly used for editing purposes. For example, I can look at my list of history in the Channel Box, select an Extrude Face command I did 20 steps ago, and actually adjust that command with the Show Manipulator Tool (T), watching the changes propagate through the steps that came after it. History also represents *active* processes, such as bound geometry to a skeleton and blend shapes. Deleting history actually deletes those processes, making any binding that has been done ineffective.

Once the geometry is bound, you will not want to delete the History of the object, because the binding depends on it.

1. Select the pelvis joint and Shift+select the remaining geometry.

2. Go to **Skin > Bind Skin > Smooth Bind > Options**.

Under Options, set the following:

Max Influences: 2

Dropoff Rate: 4

The Max Influences setting specifies the maximum number of joints that can affect each vertex. If you set this to 1, you are essentially using rigid binding. I like to tightly control the influence of painting the weight, as described in the next section, so I tend to use a low setting of 2. Feel free to experiment.

The Dropoff Rate determines the range within which vertices are affected by it. The higher the Dropoff Rate, the less influence each joint will have over distance. A Dropoff Rate of 4 is a good average number, and it can be adjusted per-joint later.

3. Click the Bind Skin button to apply the settings.

At this point, you can start rotating joints to see what kind of results your binding gave you. Don't be surprised if you get some odd results (Figure 4.15).

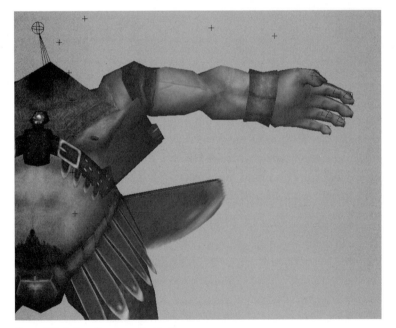

Figure 4.15 Deformation errors after binding

You can adjust the Dropoff Rate of the major joints to see if the adjustments will help the deformation. To make these adjustments, use the joint's attribute editor (Ctrl+A) under the Smooth Skin Parameters section. To make more complete fixes, you need to use painting weights.

Game Artist: Danny Ngan

Job Title Animator and 3D Artist

Studio Freelancer

Credits *ThinkTanks, BuggOut, Minigolf Maniacs, Contraptions: The Return of the Incredible Machine, Radio Control Racers, Trophy Hunting 4*

Personal Site www.dannyngan.com

Q. How and why did you get into the game industry?

A. There is something very gratifying about putting in weeks, months, years of hard work into a product and then seeing someone having the time of their lives playing that game for however long it takes them to beat it. It is not about the glory, nor is it about the money. Providing an enjoyable experience to another person is one of the best parts of working in this industry.

Q. What has been the most inspirational to you in regard to your artwork?

A. I really admire the work at Naughty Dog and Square. Naughty Dog's artists have a great sense of style and attitude in their games. The *Crash Bandicoot* series and *Jak and Daxter* are some of my favorite games of all time. Square's artists have an uncanny ability to get a hyper-real look to their games. Everything is so epic in scale, yet simple in design. I really admire what they do.

Q. What is your favorite artistic style?

A. I generally like things clean and simple. Simple lines, basic textures, limited color palettes. I do not like a lot of stuff cluttering up the essence of the work. Clean, efficient design. Everything has its place.

Q. What is your favorite kind of game?

A. I love platformers and kart-racing games. *Mario Kart, Crash Team Racing, Crash Bandicoot, Jak and Daxter, Sly Cooper, Ratchet and Clank*, just to name a few.

Q. How do you use Maya in your specific job?

A. I use Maya mostly for rigging characters, animation, and MEL scripting. I have also done general modeling (vehicles, weapons, objects, etc.) and level design with Maya. I use it pretty much for anything 3D-related.

Q. What about Maya do you like better than other 3D apps?

A. The one thing that constantly tips the scales in favor of Maya is MEL. MEL is simply the most powerful and well-integrated scripting language of all 3D programs out there. In fact, I have become so dependent on MEL that when I do have to use another 3D program, I really miss the custom scripts that I have written or downloaded. It takes me a few days to readjust to a MEL-less workflow.

Continues on next page

Painting Weights

Painting weights is probably the most time-consuming part of binding a character to a skeleton. Making certain that your joints deform the geometry smoothly requires a lot of trial and error. Painting weights can be confusing the first time you attempt it. Removing weight from one joint to add to another does not work as you might expect. Instead of directly removing weight from a specified joint, you have to add that weight to another. Although frustrating, painting weights is necessary. You need to paint the weights so that your geometry does not deform wildly when your character moves.

1. Select the body and the pelvis joint. Under the panel menus, go to **Show > Isolate Select > View Selected**.

   This will hide everything except the body geometry and the skeleton. Let's focus on the arms first.

2. Rotate the L_ShoulderPad joint about 45 degrees upward. Select the body geometry.

3. Go to **Skin > Edit Smooth Skin > Paint Skin Weights Tool > Options.** This opens the Paint Skin Weights dialog box. The body will turn black.

4. Select the L_Shoulder joint in the displayed list (Figure 4.16).

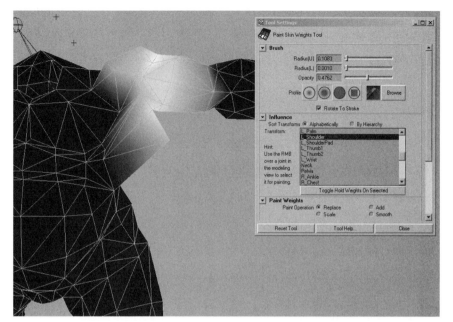

Figure 4.16 The Influence of the shoulder causes deformation.

The way painting weights works is a bit out of the ordinary. The white area of the model shows the affect of the selected joint. In order to remove weight from a joint, you have to add that area of the geometry to another joint. The underarm area of the body can be added to one of the back joints.

Set the Paint Operation setting (under the Paint Weights section) to either Replace or Add.

Note: I do not recommend using the Smooth operation. It has a tendency to scatter weight to unwanted joints all over the skeleton.

An opacity of 1.0 (under the Brush section) will paint 100 percent influence. Lower the opacity to a manageable amount, for example, 0.3. This will give you some room to work with when you paint a stroke.

5. Select the Back3 joint. The geometry's black-and-white pattern will change to display the selected joint's influence. Paint across the deformed area's vertices to add influence of the Back3 joint.

Switch back and forth between the Back3 joint and the L_Shoulder joint to adjust the weight to suit. You might have to experiment (Figure 4.17).

6. Repeat the steps for each major joint, painting weight as you go. Test the rotation of the joints and edit as necessary (Figure 4.18).

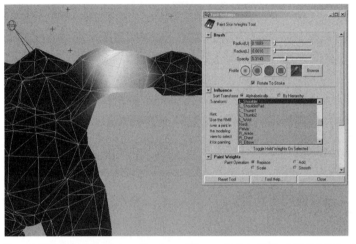

Figure 4.17 The shoulder influence after the weights are adjusted with the Paint Weights tool

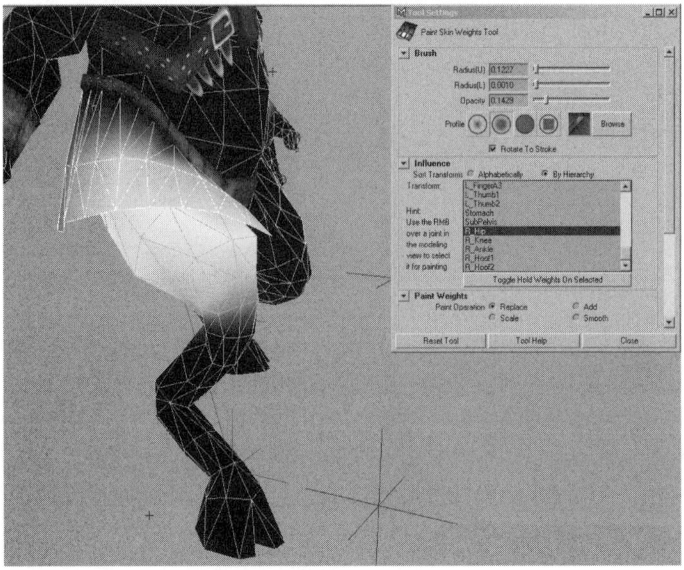

Figure 4.18 Painting the weights of the legs

Joint Rotation Limits

You'll want to limit how far some joints can rotate and in which direction they do so. For example, you don't want the elbow joint to rotate backward. To prevent this, set some limitations so Silenus will move naturally.

1. Select the L_Elbow joint. Open the Attribute Editor (Ctrl+A).

2. Under the Limit Information section, open the Rotate subsection. Rotate the elbow as far back as you want it to go.

    Your limit may vary depending on how you set the Local Rotation Axis earlier, but mine will be about three units in the Y direction.

3. Click the check box for the Max Y direction, and click the right arrow to apply the set angle to the Maximum, limiting the rotation to prohibit further rotation in the Y direction.

4. Rotate the elbow as far forward as you want it to go. Mine is about –50 units in the Y direction.

5. Click the check box for the Min Y direction, and click the left arrow to apply the set angle to the Minimum.

6. Repeat these steps for the other joints (the shoulder, wrist, and fingers) as needed.

Eye Controls

To control the movement of the eyes, you need to use an Aim Constraint. This constraint will aim the eyes at a designated object that you can then move, thereby changing the orientation of the eyes.

1. Create two new locators (**Create > Locator**). Place them about three units in front of each eye. Rename them to L_Eye_Point and R_Eye_Point.

2. Group the two locators together. Call this group Eye_Control.

3. Select the R_Eye_Point locator, and Shift+select the right eye.

4. Go to **Constrain > Aim > Options**.

    There are three columns next to the Aim Vector option. These columns represent the X, Y, and Z directions. Set these to 0, 0, 1. This sets the aim vector to run along the positive Z direction, toward the locators. Click the Add button to apply the settings. The right eye should now follow the R_Eye_Point locator.

5. Repeat Steps 1 through 4 with the left eye and the L_Eye_Point locator.

6. Display the Selection handle of the Eye_Control group, and hide (Ctrl+H) the two locators. This leaves only the selection handle visible, which makes selecting the group easier.

Rigging the Face

You're going to need a good range of facial movement to create facial expressions, lip-synch mouth movements, and build emotion with a character. There are two primary methods of doing this: using Blend Shapes and creating a Facial Skeleton.

Using Blend Shapes is a method of creating duplicates of your character's head and modeling individual facial movements into each duplicate. The original head can then be blended into these different shapes to create and animate facial expressions and lip movements. Blend Shapes can also be used for other parts of the body, such as a bicep's flex.

To create a Facial Skeleton, you use a system of joints spread over the face to animate the facial expressions as you would the rest of the body.

In both cases, the Set Driven Key process comes in handy. This process allows you to manipulate multiple objects and settings with another object. For example, if you have a couple of different blend shapes for creating a certain facial expression, you can make a single control that drives all of them at once. We will go over this in more detail after the next section.

Using Blend Shapes creates vertex animation, but be aware that not all game engines are capable of accepting vertex animation. You need to be prepared to create a facial skeleton system when needed. If you have a strict joint limit for your character, make certain you keep the joints of the face in mind when you use your allotted joints for the body.

Blend Shapes

To create blend shapes for Silenus, just follow these steps:

1. Select the head and beard geometry.

You can also select the teeth and eyes, but these objects will not be part of the blend shapes themselves. They will help us create the blend shapes in relation to their positions.

2. Duplicate the selected geometry (Ctrl+D), group these new duplicates (Ctrl+G), and move them to the side away from the model.

3. Duplicate this group again, and move the second duplicate farther to the side.

 Note: Make certain that you do not use **Modify > Freeze Transformations** on Blend Shapes objects. If you do, the blend shapes will not work correctly.

4. Adjust the vertices of the first duplicated head to close the mouth. Do not forget to adjust the beard to stay with the chin.

5. When you are ready to create another facial expression, duplicate the unmodified head to make a third duplicate. Make your new adjustments to the second duplicate.

By duplicating the unmodified head each time you start the next blend shape, you ensure that you are working with an unmodified version. Use this method to create all of the different facial expressions and mouth shapes you want to use (Figure 4.19).

> **Note:** For a great resource for the different mouth shapes used for accurate lip-synching (or *phoneme shapes*), take a look at http://www.garycmartin.com/phoneme_examples.html.

6. Once your different expressions are finished, rename them to be descriptive of their shape: Mouth_Close, Mouth_Open, etc.

7. Select all of the duplicates, and Shift+select the original head. Go to **Deform > Create Blend Shape.**

Figure 4.19 Some of Silenus's expressions

8. To control the blend shapes, go to **Window > Animation Editors > Blend Shape**. This opens a window that shows each blend shape as a slider that you can control and animate. Play with the sliders, and compound the different blend shapes together to see how you can form different expressions (Figure 4.20).

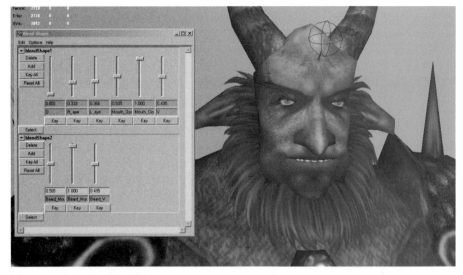

Figure 4.20 Silenus after a few drinks

9. Create blend shapes for the beard also. Blend shapes will keep the beard attached to the chin when the mouth closes and opens. Rename these shapes to make them descriptive (for example, Beard_ Mouth_Open).

You only need to worry about the blend shapes that actually change. For making eye movements and such, obviously the beard is unaffected.

Binding the Head

At this point, you can Smooth Bind the head to the skeleton. However, it might not work. Over the course of painting weights and such, some movement has probably taken place. To bind additional geometry to the skeleton, the skeleton needs to be in its *bind pose* (or original pose). The Go to Bind Pose command under the Skin menu will not work, however, with active constraints and IK handles. You may feel that you have hit a wall in your progress, but there is a way around that wall.

1. Go to **Modify > Evaluate Nodes > Ignore All**. This will block all IK handles, constraints, etc., that prevent the bind pose from being achieved.

2.   Select the pelvis joint, and go to **Skin > Go to Bind Pose**. Any skeletal movement that has taken place should snap back to its original position.

3.   Select the head geometry, and Shift+select the pelvis joint. Go to **Skin > Bind Skin > Smooth Bind**.

4.   Paint the weights of the neck and head so that they are affected by the neck and Back4 joints.

You want the base of the head geometry to match the neck opening of the body so that no seams show when the neck rotates (Figure 4.21).

Figure 4.21 The head bound to the skeleton

5.   Now that the head is bound, go to **Modify > Evaluate Nodes > Evaluate All**. This will reactivate the constraints and IK handles.

6.   Select the ears, beard, horns, teeth planes, eyes, and eyebrow planes. Shift+select the head joint. Press P to parent these elements to the head joint.

Now when you rotate the neck joint, all of these pieces should rotate with the head.

Note: If the blend shapes move incorrectly after binding, it is probably because of the *deformation order*. Blend shapes are one type of deformation, and a skeleton is another. If Maya calculates the two deformations in the wrong order, the results can be obviously incorrect. To change the deformation order, click+select the Inputs to the Selected Object button in the Status line (next to the snapping buttons) and choose All Inputs at the bottom of the menu that appears. The List of Inputs window will display all of the deformation calculations that Maya is running for the selected object, as well as their order. To change the order, middle-click and drag an item to another position in the list.

Set Driven Key

As mentioned earlier, the Set Driven Key process makes one object or setting automatically affect another. This is especially useful on the face for moving the teeth and eyebrows, and controlling the blend shapes for the beard.

Let's use Set Driven Key (SDK) to move the teeth along with the mouth when it opens and closes.

1. Deselect everything. Go to **Animate > Set Driven Key > Set > Options**. This opens the Set Driven Key window.

2. Select the lower teeth plane. In the Set Driven Key window, click the Load Driven button. In the Blend Shape animation editor, click the Select button next to the head blend shapes. In the Set Driven Key window, click the Load Driver button (Figure 4.22).

Figure 4.22 The Set Driven Key window

This procedure set the head's blend shape as the Driving object and the lower teeth plane as the Driven object. In the right side of the SDK window, you can see the different channels and attributes of the set objects.

3. In the Driver section, select the Mouth_Open blend shape. In the Driven section, select all three Translate channels and all three Rotate channels.

This designates which part of the Driver will affect which part of the Driven.

4. With the Mouth_Open blend shape set to 0, and the teeth plane in place, click the Key button in the SDK window.

5. Set the Mouth_Open blend shape to 1, opening the mouth all the way. Move and rotate the lower teeth plane into place to match the lower jaw's new position. Click the Key button in the SDK window.

Now when you raise and lower the Mouth_Open blend slider, the lower teeth plane should follow. Repeat this process for Mouth_Close and whatever other blend shapes you have that move the mouth.

Facial Skeletons

Facial skeletons are another way of rigging the face. In my opinion, the results are not quite as expressive as blend shapes can be—but they are also less work. The more joints you can have, the more expression you can give your character. This example will use seven joints.

1. Open a version of your scene from before the blend shapes (a facial skeleton will be used instead).

2. In the front view, use the Joint tool to place a joint in front of the left eye. Press Enter to deactivate the tool.

3. Duplicate (Ctrl+D or **Edit > Duplicate**) this joint, and place the duplicate over the right eye. Place more duplicates in the following places:

Between the eyes on the forehead

On the left corner of the mouth

On the right corner of the mouth

Right above the center of the chin

4. Rename the joints as:

L_Eye_Joint

R_Eye_Joint

Forehead_Joint

L_Lip_Joint

R_Lip_Joint

Jaw_Joint

5. Place a last joint in the center of the head. Name this joint Face_Joints. Parent the facial joints to this joint, creating a link (Figure 4.23).

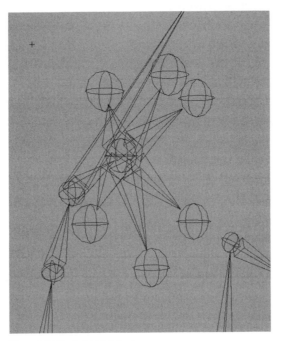

Figure 4.23 The facial joints in place

6. Parent the Face_Joints joint to the neck joint, linking it to the main skeleton.

7. Bind the head and beard to the skeleton as described earlier in the "Binding the Head" section.

This time, however, you need to paint the weights a little more meticulously to make the eyes close with the movement of the eye joints, the jaw (with beard) move with the jaw joint, etc. (Figure 4.24).

8. Parent the lower teeth plane to the Jaw_Joint. Parent the eyes, upper teeth, ears, horns, and eyebrow planes to the head joint.

Creating SDK Controls

Set Driven Key can also be used to create the animation controls for actions such as forming hand movements, blend shape combinations, or facial skeleton movements. I recommend using locators to store these types of controls.

1. Create a locator (**Create > Locator**). Rename it L_Hand_Control. Place it near the left hand.

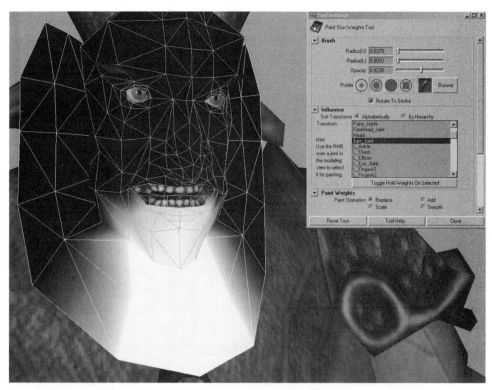

Figure 4.24 The jaw joint's weights displayed

As you can see in the Channel Box on the right side of the screen, the locator comes with standard translate, rotate, scale, and visibility channels. For ease of use, you can remove these channels.

2. Go to **Window > General Editors > Channel Control**.

The Channel Control window is divided into two main sections. The left side shows the keyable channels (the channels being displayed in the Channel Box). Non-keyable channels are on the right. By default, none of these channels are displayed in the Channel Box for animation use, but they can be used for their specific purposes. However, we want to remove channels, not add more. Select all of the channels on the left side, and click the Move>> button to make these channels nonkeyable.

The Channel Box for the locator is now empty and ready for you to use.

3. Go to **Modify > Add Attribute**.

The Add Attribute window opens. This window allows you to create your own keyable channels. Your goal is to create a control that will make Silenus's hand form a fist for gripping the sword.

4. Set the following:

- **Attribute Name:** Fist
- **Minimum:** 0
- **Maximum:** 10
- **Default:** 0

By setting a minimum of 0 and maximum of 10, you made the control a slider between 0 and 10 with the default value set to 0.

5. Click OK to apply the settings.

In the Channel Box, you will now find a new channel called Fist.

6. Open the Set Driven Key window. Load the locator as the Driver. Load the L_Thumb1, L_FingerA1, L_FingerA2, L_FingerB1, and L_FingerB2 joints as the Driven (Figure 4.25).

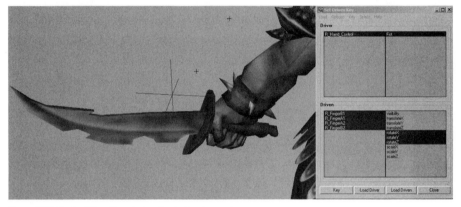

Figure 4.25 The Set Driven Key window for the hand control

7. With the Fist channel set to 0 and the finger joints at their default location, click the Key button.

8. Set Fist to 10. Rotate the fingers to make a gripping fist around the sword (you can place the sword in the hand to guide you). Click the Key button again.

Note: You can use the channels in the Channel Box as a slider by left-clicking on the name of the channel and middle-mouse dragging in your scene.

Now when you slide the Fist channel between 0 and 10, the fingers of the hand should open and close, forming a fist. Repeat these steps to form more hand movements as needed for your project. Create new keyable attributes for each movement. Feel free to form an R_Hand_Control using the same method.

9. Parent the locators to their respective wrist joints so they move with the character.

Sword Constraints

You have a couple of different options you can use to control the character's sword. You will probably want to be able to have Silenus sheathe his sword and draw it when needed.

One way to do this is to actually have two swords—one parented to the hand, and the other parented to the sheath. You can then key the visibility of the two swords to "switch" between the two. However, this method is not very efficient because you now have two swords and, therefore, double the number of polygons for the swords.

For this example, you will constrain the sword to both the hand and a sheath position on Silenus's back. By using this method, you can then key the constraints between these two points and switch between the two positions.

1. Create a locator, and point snap it to the palm joint. Rename it to Hand_ Constraint.

2. Place the sword in the hand, press Insert to enter pivot mode, and point snap the pivot of the sword to the locator. Press Insert again to exit pivot mode.

3. Select the locator, and Shift+select the sword. Go to **Constrain** > **Point**. Next, use **Constrain** > **Orient**.

The Orient constraint will drive the rotation of the sword by rotating the locator. Rotate the locator to fit the sword in the hand as you want it.

4. Create a new locator, and place it near the right shoulder on the back of the character. Rename it Back_Constraint.

5. Select the new locator, and Shift+select the sword. Again, apply Point and Orient constraints.

The sword should now appear halfway between the two locators. This is because both locators currently have an equal amount of influence on the sword.

6. Select the sword. In the Channel Box under the Shapes section, you will find two new items: Sword_pointConstraint1 and Sword_orientConstraint1. Clicking either of these will open up the available attributes in the Channel Box. The bottom two show the influence amounts. A value of 1 equals 100 percent influence. A value of 0 equals no influence.

7. Enter **0** for both of the hand constraints, and enter **1** for the back constraints.

Now, 100 percent of the influence on the sword is placed on the Back_Constraint.

8. Rotate the Back_Constraint locator to orient the sword properly on the back as if it were sheathed (Figure 4.26).

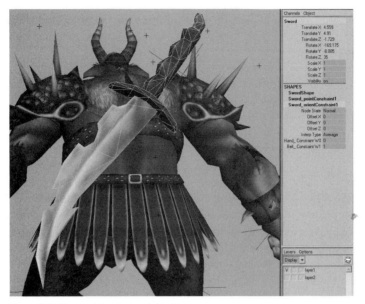

Figure 4.26 The sword sheathed on the back

Switching the constraints of the hand and back from 0 to 1 and from 1 to 0 will now change the position of the sword between the two locators.

9. Parent the Hand_Constraint locator to the palm joint of the hand to keep the sword with the hand's position. Parent the Back_Constraint locator to the Back3 joint. Silenus should now be ready for action!

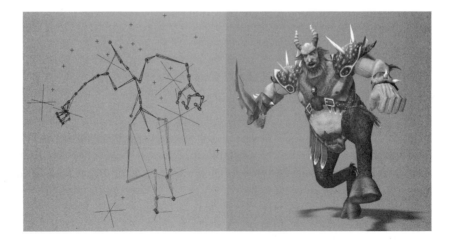

Maya in Games: Homeworld 2

Genre 3D Real-Time Strategy

Developer Relic Entertainment

Publisher Sierra

Platform PC

Homeworld 2 is a beautiful game. It is fun to just zoom in and admire all of the different space-ships and huge motherships that make up the player's navy. Utilizing a fantastically realized Level of Detail (LOD) system, the ships in the game increase in polycount and texture resolution as the player's camera view gets closer. The particle effects of each ship's attacks and special moves are also very impressive. The environments are nicely detailed with particle-based nebulas and other space matter.

I definitely recommend studying this game for its impressive sense of scale and level of detail, as well as the lighting and particle effects. The slick visual style of its interface is also worth noting.

Animation

With the animation controls in place, the character can come to life through movement. Just as 2D animation is done in cartoons, 3D animation with Maya software is done by setting keyframes at specific poses and adjusting how those poses blend (or interpolate) from one to another. In this chapter, you will learn how to animate games by using animation clips that blend together for seamless transitions. You will also be introduced to other tips and tricks of the trade.

Chapter Contents

Creating a Character Set

In general, you animate a character by creating poses and manipulating the character's skeleton. To do this, you set *keyframes* (or key poses) at certain points along the timeline.

Note that animation can be handled in extremely varied ways from project to project based on the different game engines involved. In this chapter, you will use the Trax Editor (**Window > Animation Editors > Trax Editor**) and *character sets*; however, not all game engines use such things. The process of animating, on the other hand, is pretty standard.

A character set is a way for Maya to put all of a character's animation controls together under one handle so you don't have to hunt through a skeleton looking for a missing joint. To use the Trax Editor (which will be discussed later), character sets must be used.

1. Once you have finished the rigged model from the previous chapter, open it or navigate on the CD to Tutorials/Chapter 4/Character_Rigging/Scenes/ Steps and copy the 05_Final_wblendshapes.mb file to the project directory's Scenes folder on your hard drive.

2. Select the following joints: Pelvis, Back1, Back2, Back3, Back4, and Neck.

3. With all of these joints, groups, and locators selected, go to the Animation module (F2), **Character > Create Character Set > Options**. In the options, change the name to **Silenus_Set**. Under the Attributes section, place a check in Scale, Visibility, and Dynamic. Click the Create Character Set button.

This has created a character set called Silenus_Set that contains the Translate and Rotate channels of all of the previously selected joints, groups, and locators. You can select this character set in the Outliner and see that all of the channel controls that have been combined under the one set. (**Window > Outliner** displays a list of all items in your scene.)

Editing the Character Set

With the previous character set options, the Translate and Rotate channels of each of the selected objects are displayed in the Channel Box. However, you may want to add a set of controls, such as the head's Blend Shape controls, to this list.

1. Open the Blend Shape window (**Window > Animation Editors > Blend Shape**).

2. Press the Select button next to the head Blend Shape sliders. This selects the blend shape. You can see the different Blend Shape controls not only in the Blend Shape window but in the Channel Box. Select the Blend Shape channels.

3. Go to **Character > Add to Character Set**. This adds the Blend Shape controls to the character set.

Some of the channels currently in the Silenus_Set, such as the translate controls for the joints, are not needed. (They will be rotated only during animation.) To keep the work area clean, remove these unnecessary channels.

4. Select the Silenus_Set character set. In the Channel Box, select the Translate X, Y, and Z channels of all of the joints currently in the set, except the Pelvis joint.

5. Go to **Character > Remove from Character Set**.

    This effectively removes the selected channels from the character set.

Creating a Subcharacter Set

The next step is to add the joints and controls of the hands and arms to the character set. At this point, however, the list in the Channel Box is getting rather long. To help organize the set of controls, you can create a *subcharacter set* (or subset) for each arm. A subcharacter set is a grouping of character set controls under a heading that is under the main character set's hierarchy.

1. Select the following joints: L_ShoulderPad, L_Shoulder, L_Elbow, L_Forearm, L_Wrist, L_FingerA1 and 2, L_FingerB1 and 2, and L_Thumb1.

2. Go to **Character > Create Subcharacter Set > Options**. In the options, name the set **LArm**. Under the Subcharacter Set Attributes, make sure the following are checked:

    No Translate

    No Scale

    No Visibility

    Click the Create Subcharacter Set button.

    This creates a subset called LArm that has the rotation channels of the previously selected joints. As a subset, it is under the hierarchy of the main Silenus_Set character set. Next, you will add the Fist channel of the L_Hand_Control locator.

3. At the bottom of the screen, make certain the LArm subcharacter set is the active character set (Figure 5.1).

4. Select the L_Hand_Control locator. Click the Fist channel control, and go to **Character > Add to Character Set**.

    This adds the Fist control to the designated LArm subcharacter set. Set the Silenus_Set character set as the active character set (otherwise, another subset will be placed under the LArm subset). Repeat these steps on the right arm, leg joints, and locators to create a RArm, RLeg, and LLeg subset.

    Remember, not all game engines use character sets this way. For example, I just worked on a project for which animations were set up in their own files without any sort of joint organization. We just had to make certain that the animations would blend properly by starting and ending the animation on the same pose. The method you use really depends on the project. Your art lead will tell you the particulars that your job requires. Creating character sets like this, though, can definitely speed up most workflows.

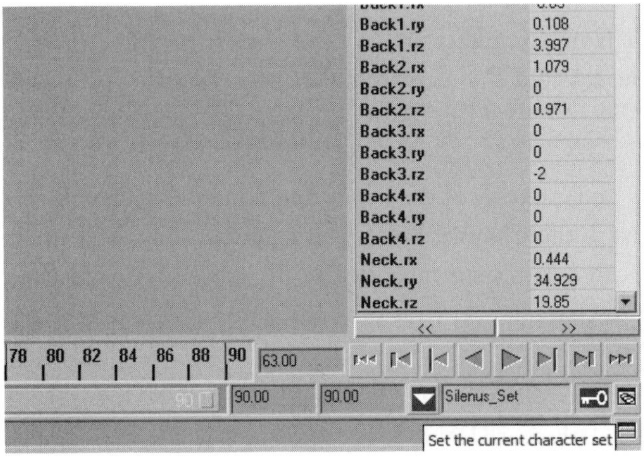
Back1.ry 0.108
Back1.rz 3.997
Back2.rx 1.079
Back2.ry 0
Back2.rz 0.971
Back3.rx 0
Back3.ry 0
Back3.rz -2
Back4.rx 0
Back4.ry 0
Back4.rz 0
Neck.rx 0.444
Neck.ry 34.929
Neck.rz 19.85
78 80 82 84 86 88 90
63.00
90.00
90.00
Silenus_Set
Set the current character set

Figure 5.1 Set the Current Character Set button next to the range slider

Now that you have your character set, you can animate Silenus normally (or through the character set's channels) and eventually create what are known as animation *clips* for the Trax Editor. A clip is an animation that can be easily manipulated in the Trax Editor, allowing you to shorten or lengthen the timing as well as stack and blend between clips. You can start by animating something simple, such as a few sword swings so that Silenus can attack.

Creating a Quality Animation

Creating animation is really quite simple. Making a *quality* animation, on the other hand, takes a lot of practice. *Emphasis* and *timing* are two of the main focuses of this section.

Emphasis refers mostly to exaggeration and dynamic poses. In animation for games as well as other media, you almost always want to exaggerate movements and actions to make sure that what the character or creature is doing is both interesting and "readable" on the player's screen. In a football game like *Madden*, the player needs very obvious visual feedback in order to accurately react to the opponent and confirm that their actions are performing properly. Spending a lot of time on an action animation that the player won't notice is a waste of time and resources. In the action game *The Lord of the Rings*, the warrior dwarf Gimli swings his axe in large sweeping moves with bounding leaps that are visually very obvious and impressive. If his attacks were not so noticeable and exciting, the game would quickly become boring.

When dialogue is spoken, a character needs to visually emote what he is saying. He needs body language and definite emphasis of emotional highs and lows. Otherwise, the character can come across as very stiff and dull.

Timing is also important. Inserting secondary motions, such as *anticipation* (secondary movement before a primary movement) and *follow-through* (secondary movement after a primary movement), adds a lot to fluid motion. Pauses and overlaps between movements emphasize certain poses to help make an animation more "readable" on screen. When Silenus attacks with his sword, for example, you want him to pause slightly before the release of the swinging motion to really convey his strength and mass.

Of course, lots of different techniques and methods are used for animating games and film. None are necessarily wrong. Most game animations require certain aspects that are not typical for most other mediums, however. A game is, after all, an interactive medium that reacts to input from the player. The player's press of a button triggers an animation to take place.

In many cases, you'll need to use an *idle animation* from which all other animations blend. An idle animation is what the character does when it is standing still with no input from the player. When a button is pressed (or some other stimulus such as an enemy attack), an animation will trigger, blending from this idle sequence to a new animation and conveying the new action. It can then blend back into an idle or to another animation. Many modern game engines include animation blending that helps with this blending process. This book will focus mostly on blending from one animation to another.

Animation Reference

On the CD, you can navigate to the `Video/Animation Reference` folder to find a variety of filmed martial arts moves performed by my friend Arvee Garde.

Animation reference is invaluable for getting realistic movements. However, as you will discover in the following tutorials, strictly copying reference video motions can result in unexciting or even inappropriate movement. For example, Arvee does not have near the mass that Silenus does. Mimicking Arvee's movements exactly would result in a movement that would not look natural on Silenus's monstrous form. But first, you can bring these videos into Maya for ease of use.

1. The first animation tutorial will use the `move1` files from the CD. Copy `move1_front_small.avi` and `move1_side_small.avi` to your project directory's Sourceimages folder on your hard drive.

2. In Maya, create a new polygon plane with the following options (**Create > Polygon Primitives > Plane > Options**):

   Width: 2.4 units

   Height: 3.2 units

   Subdivisions Along Width: 1

   Subdivisions Along Height: 1

   Axis: Z

   The `move1_front_small.avi` has a resolution of 240 × 320 pixels. Creating a polygon plane of 2.4 × 3.2 units creates a plane with the same resolution ratio so that our video will not be stretched or compressed. Setting the axis to Z will cause the flat surface of the plane to orient itself in the Z direction, along with the character. You can scale the plane to match the size of the character.

3. Right-click on the plane. In the marking menu that opens, go to **Materials > Assign New Material > Lambert**.

   This applies a new Lambert material to the plane and opens the Attribute Editor.

4. Click the Mapping button next to the color attribute. In the Create Render Node window, choose Movie.

5. In the Movie attributes that now open, click on the folder icon next to the Image Name text box and open `move1_front_small.avi`. Check the Use Image Sequence check box.

Note: Make sure you have the latest DivX video codec installed for the video to work.

Now, when you "scrub" left or right with the dynamic slider of the Timeline, you should see the video play on the plane (Figure 5.2).

Take a look at the video. You should note a couple of things. First of all, as mentioned earlier, Arvee does not have the same kind of body mass as Silenus. He goes through the movements very smoothly with no real pauses between swings and such. For a game, you will want to spice the movement up a bit to make it more visually exciting and interesting. Essentially, the movement you end up with should not be exactly like the provided video. You should use the video as a reference for the movement only.

Figure 5.2 The reference animation in the scene

To help get your feet wet, try to match Arvee's movement pose-to-pose. Then, you can go back and retime and reemphasize the animation to make it more game-like.

Note: Before beginning the animation, make sure your Timeline is set to a playback speed of 30 frames per second (fps). Click the Animation Preferences button next to the key icon near the Range slider. The Settings/Preferences window will open to the Timeline section. If 30 fps is not available for the playback speed options, click on the Settings section in the list on the left. Change the Time option to NTSC (30 fps). Click the Save button to apply the settings.

Making an Attack Animation

You can begin by matching Arvee's movements as close as possible, pose-to-pose. The poses you will match for the first move are shown in Figure 5.3.

Frame 1

Frame 22

Frame 33

Frame 45

Frame 58

Frame 90

Figure 5.3 The major poses

You can see that the first and last poses are the same. This will allow the next animation that is triggered in a game to start seamlessly.

1. At frame 1, make the following changes, matching the pose in the video reference. (Depending on how you set the Local Rotation Axis in the previous chapter, your settings may vary. The settings should work fine if you're using the file from the CD for this exercise.) For easy key setting, press Shift+W to key all Translate channels and Shift+E to key all Rotation channels.

Body Part	Settings
Pelvis	Translate X: 0 Y: 6 Z: -1.7
Pelvis	Rotate X: 0 Y: 28 Z: 0

Body Part	Settings
Back1	Rotate X: -7 Y: 0.2 Z: 0.7
Back2	Rotate X: 2 Y: 0 Z: 1.8
Back3	Rotate X: 0 Y: 0 Z: -2
Neck	Rotate X: -2.2 Y: -18.5 Z: 8
L_ShoulderPad	Rotate X: 9.5 Y: 25.5 Z: 21.7
L_Shoulder	Rotate X: -25 Y: 13.8 Z: -27.5
L_Elbow	Rotate X: 0 Y: -66.5 Z: 0
L_Forearm	Rotate X: -37 Y: 0 Z: 0
L_Knee_Locator	Translate X: 4 Y: 1.8 Z: 2.2
R_ShoulderPad	Rotate X: 21.5 Y: 13.7 Z: 13.5
R_Shoulder	Rotate X: -2.2 Y: 10.8 Z: -7.5
R_Elbow	Rotate X: 0 Y: -68.5 Z: 0
R_Forearm	Rotate X: -2.2 Y: 0 Z: 0
R_Wrist	Rotate X: -1.5 Y: 17 Z: 10.5
R_Knee_Locator	Translate X: -3.3 Y: 2 Z: 2.8
L_Hand_Control and R_Hand_Control	Fist: 10
L_Foot	Translate X: 0 Y: 0 Z: -2.4
L_Foot	Rotate X: 0 Y: 14.5 Z: 0
R_Foot	Translate X: 0.8 Y: 0 Z: 0.7
R_Foot	Rotate X: 0 Y: 22.5 Z: 0
Eye_Control	Translate X: 0.2 Y: 0.1 Z: 0.7

Note: Avoid pressing the **S** key, which sets a keyframe on all channels. Doing so would create unnecessary keyframes for unchanging channels, which would be inefficient. However, you can easily remove keys that have no effect by using **Edit** > **Delete by Type** > **Static Channels**. This removes keyframes that do not change and have no effect on the animation.

With these settings, you can achieve a result like Figure 5.4. This will be the basic pose that all of your animations will start and end on. Feel free to adjust the facial blend shapes however you like.

Notice that for twisting the wrist, you use the forearm joint. For bending the wrist, you use the wrist joint. Twist your own arm, and you can see how the forearm drives the movement. You can use a forearm joint to simulate this movement.

Figure 5.4 Matching Arvee's pose at frame 1

2. In the Timeline, track to frame 22, which is the next major pose of the movement. Once more, you should move and rotate the joints to match the pose as close as possible. Here are my settings for the right arm. Remember to set a key for each new entry.

Body Part	Settings
R_ShoulderPad	Rotate X: 48.8 Y: -4 Z: 26.2
R_Shoulder	Rotate X: 20.1 Y: -2.9 Z: -14
R_Elbow	Rotate X: 0 Y: -87 Z: 0
R_Forearm	Rotate X: -30.5 Y: 0 Z: 0
R_Wrist	Rotate X: -16.4 Y: 20.2 Z: 23.7

 Note: If a joint's previously set rotation limit prevents you from rotating a joint the way you want, feel free to adjust the limit settings in the joint's Attribute Editor, as described in Chapter 4.

Using the video reference, adjust the other joints of the body to match it as closely as possible (Figure 5.5). Keep in mind that Silenus has a bit more mass than Arvee, so it may not be possible to match his articulation exactly without Silenus's body deforming in unsatisfactory ways.

Figure 5.5 The next pose at frame 22

At this point, I will not list the settings for each pose. I think you get the idea and, as stated previously, my settings will probably not apply correctly to your model. So, take what you've learned so far, and apply your own settings to get the desired results. Feel free to reference the files provided on the CD if you run into any problems.

3. The next major pose is at frame 33. Repeat the previous steps. Rotate the joints, position the knee locators and feet, adjust the blend shapes, etc. to match the pose. Repeat for frames 45 and 58 (Figure 5.6).

For the last pose at frame 90, you'll want to mimic the pose at frame 1 so that your poses will blend together to the next animation.

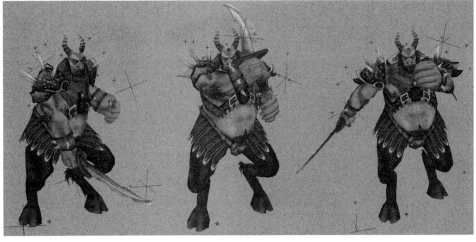

<table>
<tr><td>Frame 33</td><td>Frame 45</td><td>Frame 58</td></tr>
</table>

Figure 5.6 Poses for frames 33, 45, and 58

4. Go to Frame 1. Middle-click and drag the Timeline to frame 90.

This moves the Timeline forward without actually progressing forward in time. Now, by keying all of the joints, locators, etc. in their current positions, you can essentially copy the keys from frame 1 to frame 90.

You have essentially created a simple attack animation. You used an animation reference and matched Arvee's movement pose-to-pose. However, you can definitely improve the character's movement by making better use of timing and emphasis.

Creating Emphasis

To really emphasize the movements and make them more game-like, take your current poses and exaggerate them. Make them grandiose and obvious. Exaggerating movements makes them seem fiercer and more "readable" to the player.

Rotate the pelvis, back, and neck joints, giving the character much more range of motion in the spine. Lift his pelvis up as if were climbing up for more power, and lower it down when he goes in for the kill. Do the same for the other poses. Even go so far as having the character take a step forward or backward so that he keeps his balance. If you move his feet, make sure you go about half way between the two keys and lift the leg up so his foot does not drag along the ground. If a character has one foot off the ground, make sure you move his pelvis so that it is over his planted foot, giving him a good sense of balance. My exaggerated poses are shown in Figure 5.7.

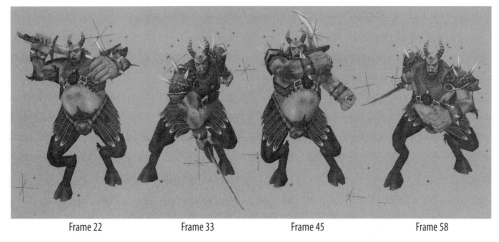

| Frame 22 | Frame 33 | Frame 45 | Frame 58 |

Figure 5.7 Modified poses with much more emphasis and exaggeration

Modify Timing in the Trax Editor

Timing can be modified in many ways, ranging from editing individual keys to creating animation clips and modifying them in the Trax Editor. We will go over the latter. Select the Silenus_Set character set from the Outliner (**Window** > **Outliner**).

1. Open the Trax Editor from **Window** > **Animation Editors** > **Trax Editor**. With the character set selected, go to **Create** > **Clip** in the Trax Editor. Five blue bars, representing the character set and the four subsets, will appear.

2. Go to frame 22. This is where the first windup of the sword ends and the first sword swing begins. Select the five clips, and go to **Edit** > **Split** in the Trax Editor menus. Repeat the split for frames 33, 45, and 58 (Figure 5.8).

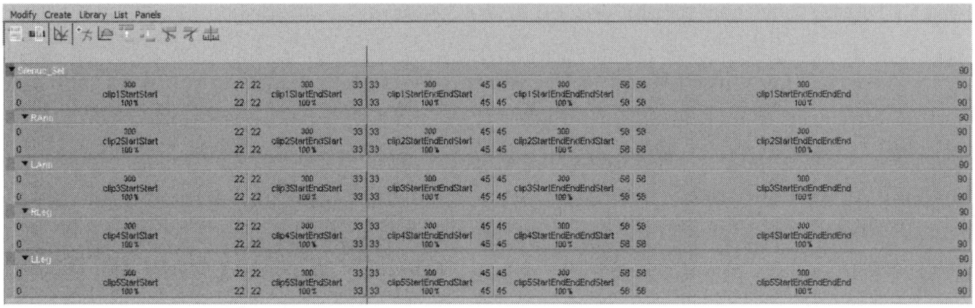

Figure 5.8 The split clips in the Trax Editor

Note: Double-click the clip names to rename them. Name them descriptively (for example, LLeg_Swing1, RArm_Windup2, etc.).

These splits have divided the large clips into smaller clip segments that can be individually edited. Because Silenus is a rather large character, you need to adjust the timing to make his movements a bit more lumbering and not quite so swift. As he is now, his pose at frame 33 goes by too quickly.

3. Go to frame 30. Select the five clips that make up the swing section of movement, and create a new split.

4. Select all of the clips after this section. With multiple clips selected, you can see a white arrow on either side of the selection and a white circle in the middle. The white circle handle allows you to move the clips as a group, and the arrows allow you to scale them. Move the clips to the right about five frames.

5. You now have a gap between the first sword swing and the second windup clips. Select the clips that make up the end of the sword swing, and use the right arrow to scale this clip to fill in the gap (Figure 5.9).

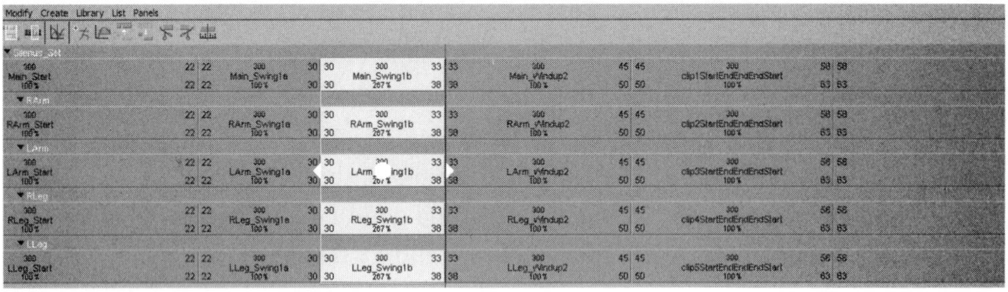

Figure 5.9 Extending the first swing animation clip

Now, the last three frames of the swing have been extended to run over eight frames. However, in my animation, the left leg takes a step backward during this clip. With the adjustments, the step was extended over eight frames and can look like it is hovering for an unnecessary length of time. To make the leg plant on the ground and actually stay planted for about 10 frames, adjust the LLeg subset clips by themselves.

6. Click and drag the bottom-right corner of the first sword swing clip, and scale it back to frame 33, so that it once again lasts only three frames.

7. Grab the bottom-left corner of the next LLeg clip (the beginning of the windup for the next swing), and drag it forward so that it does not start until frame 44. Now, the left leg's position remains stationary for 11 frames (Figure 5.10).

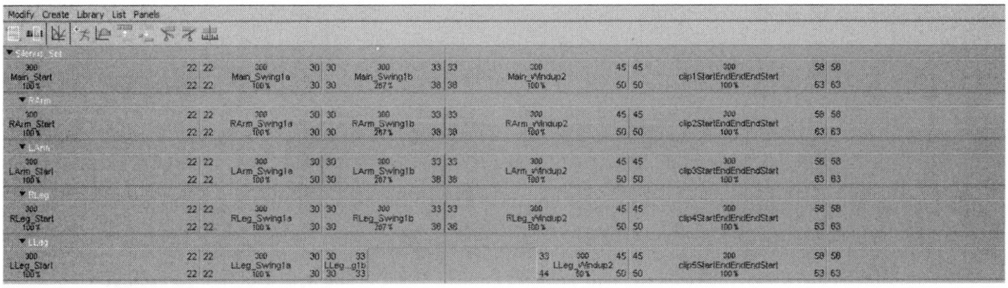

Figure 5.10 Adjusting the left leg's timing

When you play the animation now, the first swing lingers a few frames before beginning the next swing's windup animation. This gives the character a better sense of power and bulk. You'll want to repeat these steps for the next windup, making the windup linger a bit before beginning the next swing.

Additional Timing

Next, we will do some additional tweaks to further adjust the timing of the animation.

1. Go to frame 47 (or, if yours is different, about three frames before the end of the windup clips). Create a new split here in all the clips except the LLeg clip, which you already handled in the previous section.

2. Move all of the clips after the windup further down the Timeline about four or five frames.

3. Scale the new half of the windup clips to fill in the created gap.

At this point of the animation, you can start making minor adjustments to the timing as you see fit. For instance, I think the second swing of the sword lasts a couple of frames too long. You can click and drag the bottom-right corner of the clips and shorten them about two frames to the left. Then move the clips after that section to the left to fill the gaps.

Secondary Motion

Secondary motion, as mentioned earlier, is movement that is generally the result of another movement. Such movements are usually very subtle, but they can add a lot to an animation's believability. When such elements are in place, the viewer will barely notice them; however, their absence can stand out loud and clear. Some examples of common elements that should exhibit secondary motion include:

- A long tail
- Antennae
- Long ears

- Loose clothing
- Pinned objects (such as medals or a gun in a holster, etc.)

Note: If you ever need to retime an animation on a keyframe-by-keyframe basis, as opposed to an entire clip, select the clip in question in the Trax Editor and go to **View > Graph Anim Curves...** . This opens the Graph Editor (**Window > Animation Editors > Graph Editor**) with the selected clip's keyframes loaded onto its timeline. By doing this, you can move individual keyframes in the clip and have explicit control. Another method is to select the clip in question, right-click on it, and choose Activate Keys. The keyframes will appear on the Time slider again, allowing you to adjust them normally.

Much of Silenus's body and armor are bound directly to the skeleton, which does not leave much room for secondary movement. However, he does have long, floppy ears and his shoulder pads.

1. Make certain the ear and shoulder pad pivot points are placed correctly. The ear pivots should be where the ear meets the head. The shoulder pad pivots can be point snapped to their respective ShoulderPad joints.

2. At their current, default positions, set keys (Shift+E to key the rotation only) at the beginning and end of the animation so that the motion will blend without difficulty.

Because the ears are the long, droopy kind, you can have them bounce in relation to Silenus's movements. When Silenus rises up rapidly, have the ears droop down. When he lowers his body for the first swing, raise the ears.

You can animate the shoulder pads similarly. As Silenus rapidly moves up and down, have the shoulder pads continue that movement. Silenus rises up and rapidly swings down; the shoulder pad swings open until it catches up with the downward movement on the upswing, etc. (Figure 5.11).

Figure 5.11 The shoulder pad and ear display secondary motion.

Artist Profile: Jon Jones

Job Title Artist

Studio Liquid Development

Credits *Gore*, *Yourself Fitness*, *Coca-Cola NCAA Madness*, *The Sims 2*, *Mythica*, *Ultima X Odyssey*, *SWAT 4*

Studio Site www.liquiddevelopment.com

Personal Site http://shineypoo.blogspot.com/

Q. How and why did you get into the game industry?

A. I was raised with computers, and ever since I could operate one without drooling on the keyboard, I've been involved in art. Naturally, I've always loved video games. Sometime in 1997, I saw a copy of *PC Gamer* with *Duke Nukem Forever* on the cover, and I saw a screenshot of one of the game's models inside the 3D application. I realized that I actually *had* that application, and it dawned on me that I could make art for games too. The convergence of two things I loved completely blew me away, and I knew I had to do it, right then, immediately.

I began creating free modifications for *Quake*, then for *Quake 2*. I eventually made a name for myself in the mod community and began taking various freelance jobs. In 2001, I got my first contract job working on a real game, working for 4D Rulers as Lead Character Artist on their first person shooter, *Gore*. I designed and modeled a dozen player models for the game and various environment objects. After that, I kept doing freelance work until I came across Liquid Development, an art studio, where I am currently employed.

Q. Describe your role at your studio.

A. I am an artist specializing in using Maya for characters, but I also do environment art. Since Liquid Development is an art studio, I switch projects every few weeks, so I have to rapidly learn the development pipeline for new projects, adjust to their art style, and be on call to use whatever applications the client needs.

Q. What has been the most inspirational to you in regard to your artwork?

A. I love that the right amount of sweat, tears, and elbow grease can get you anywhere. I started out in the *Quake* mod scene very early, and I have seen a handful of artists start where I was and become tremendously talented based on their hard work and relentless drive to improve themselves. It is a quality I share with them, and seeing where they began and how far they have pushed themselves is immensely inspiring. It makes me keep pushing harder and harder to improve myself and my art to get that kind of gratification—the feeling of pure achievement.

Continues

Artist Profile: Jon Jones *(Continued)*

Q. What is your favorite artistic style?

A. I am very fond of exaggerated, stylized realism. The *Unreal* games are a great example of this, and so is one particular artist named Mike James, who creates the sexiest women in the world in this style.

Q. What is your favorite kind of game?

A. I am hopelessly in love with hack-n-slash role-playing games. *Diablo 2* and *Dungeon Siege* are two of my favorite games of all time. They appeal to two very specific primal needs of mine:

1. The need for gradual improvement through increasingly difficult challenges.

2. The need to collect treasure chests full of cool trinkets!

Q. How do you use Maya in your specific job?

A. It depends on the job. For *Mythica*, I was modeling and rigging mythological creature models. For *The Sims 2*, I was rigging, UV mapping, and optimizing existing models to create lower-polygon level-of-detail models for 75 Sims characters. For *Coca-Cola NCAA Madness*, I was modeling, rigging, and animating a crowd for a basketball stadium.

Q. What about Maya do you like better than other 3D apps?

A. Its modeling tools and character setup are second to none. Its flexibility and ease of customization also puts it head and shoulders above the rest. I am confident that if I cannot find a feature in Maya, I can either find or create a MEL script that will do exactly what I want. There is simply nothing else out there with that level of control.

Q. Which Maya tool could you not live without?

A. The Box primitive! Just kidding… but not really. The Split Polygon tool is a most beautiful and perfect creation, and I have not seen it pulled off this well in any other package.

Q. What advice might you have for the up-and-coming game artist?

A. Develop a sense of who is worthwhile when you are getting critiques of your work. People that say your work is perfect and you do not need to improve hurt you by holding you back. If they cared about you, they would help you grow. Understand that people who carefully critique your work *do* care about you. They show it by investing their time and effort in you. Treat them with respect. The less you want to hear what they are saying, the more you need to hear it. The truth hurts. Embrace it and grow.

As I said, the effect is very subtle—but you should see how much it adds to the overall movement. Another form of secondary motion is *overlapping motion*. Overlapping motion helps remove the robotic, synchronized movement that tends to take place when animating. The left arm is one of the larger areas where you can put this technique into action. Right now, it is moving at the same time the sword arm moves. You can overlap its motion some, so that it is the driving force behind the motion. Simulate Silenus throwing his arm around to build the swinging momentum he needs for his attack.

3.   In the Trax Editor, select the LArm's first four clips, and move them about seven frames to the left. As a result, the left arm begins its motion earlier during the first swing of the sword.

4.   Move the remaining LArm clips about seven frames to the right. This causes the left arm's motion to begin later during the second swing of the sword.

5.   Scale the beginning, middle, and end clips to reform with the rest of the animation and fill the gap.

There you have it! Your first animation completed with Silenus. On the CD, navigate to Video/Model_Stages/Animation1 to see the different animation passes. (You can also find videos of other project stages on the CD.)

Pass1: We matched the movement of our video reference, pose-to-pose.

Pass2: We reemphasized the movement, adding exaggeration and excitement to the motion.

Pass3: We retimed the movement, adding readability, weight, and power to the animation.

Pass4: We added secondary motion, the bounce of the shoulder pads and ears and the overlap of the left arm.

Idle Animation

Now that you know the general workflow for creating an animation, you can learn about the different types of animations you can expect to create in a typical game situation. *Idle animations* create movement that takes place when there is no input from the player. Such movement keeps a character from suddenly becoming a static statue, and it maintains some sense of life. Depending on what kind of game you are working on, you may need to make quite a few different idle animations—an attack idle (idle while in combat), a passive idle (idle while not in combat), conversing idle (idle while speaking with another character), etc. Each type of idle animation can have multiple variations so that the same one is not seen as often, thereby giving the character some visual variety.

Some games, such as in *Super Mario 64,* even make special idles specifically for people to find if they take no action for a specified amount of time. If you leave Mario idling, he will eventually break into an animation that shows him stretching and yawning until finally he lies down to take a nap. In other games, the main character might start tapping his foot and looking back toward the camera as if goading the player to make an action.

Most of the time, however, idle animations should be very subtle. As an attack idle for Silenus, you could have him warily bobbing to and fro, watching for his opponent to make a move against him.

Forward Movement

Let's try another attack move, and apply what you have learned in this chapter. You can try the move3_front_small.avi video reference. This move is a bit more complicated than the first one, as it has the character take a step or two forward during the attack.

When walking or running in a game, the animation itself generally does not actually move the character forward or back. The animation will actually have the character running or walking in place while the game engine itself moves the character around during gameplay based on input from the player. In the following example, you can see that the box does not move in relation to the Y axis (the thick vertical line). However, the animation of the legs simulate forward movement. The specific requirements of your project will, of course, be made known to you by your Art Director.

Frame 33   Frame 49   Frame 57

Before getting started, remember to make the first and last poses of your animation the same as in the first attack so that you can blend between them without trouble. In Figure 5.12, you can see Arvee's major poses.

Frame 25

Frame 33

Frame 41

Frame 49

Frame 57

Frame 63

Figure 5.12 The major poses of the video reference

Next, we will go through our first pass at the animation, matching Arvee pose-to-pose. This is a good example of how matching pose-to-pose (or even motion capture) does not necessarily give satisfactory results without further passes. In this example, the sword cuts right through Silenus's arm when matching the reference (Figure 5.13).

Frame 25 Frame 33 Frame 41

Frame 49 Frame 57 Frame 63

Figure 5.13 Matching the reference pose-to-pose

For the next step, you need to exaggerate and emphasize the movements to make it more dynamic and eye-catching. Because of Silenus's greater size, adjust the movements accordingly to make sure you don't introduce errors, such as the sword intersecting the body. (See Figure 5.14.)

Frame 25

Frame 33

Frame 41

Frame 49

Frame 57

Frame 63

Figure 5.14 The exaggerated poses

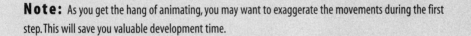

Note: As you get the hang of animating, you may want to exaggerate the movements during the first step. This will save you valuable development time.

Motion Capture

Motion capture is a process you may have seen demonstrated in behind-the-scenes videos from many feature films and games. The technique utilizes an array of cameras and computer equipment to capture the motion of an actor and automatically create that motion on a skeleton in the computer. While motion capture can be a great time saver, it is seldom the end of the animation process. The process of creating emphasis and adjusting the timing still remains. Think of motion capture as the ultimate pose-to-pose first pass of an animation.

After you have finished exaggerating and emphasizing, you can retime and enforce "readability" by using clips in the Trax Editor. Make sure that the character moves naturally and not too fast or too slow (Figure 5.15).

Finally, add secondary motion to add that little bit of believability that might be lacking otherwise. You can animate the shoulder pads and Silenus's ears. You should also add overlapping motion so that the body does not move in synch.

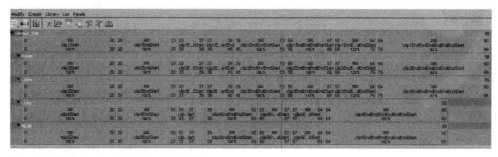

Figure 5.15 Retiming the animation in the Trax Editor

Blending Between Clips

Now that you have two attack animations and an idle animation, you can try to blend between the clips in a single file. First, you need to export your animation clips.

1. Open the Trax Editor.

2. Go to **File** > **Export Clip….** Name the animation something descriptive, such as move2.ma.

3. Repeat Steps 1 and 2 for the idle animation, naming it `idle.ma`.

4. Open the first completed animation, and open the Trax Editor.

5. Go to the next frame after the end of the animation.

6. Make certain that the Silenus_Set character set is active.

7. In the Trax Editor, go to **File > Import Clip to Characters...**. Choose the `idle.ma` file.

The idle clip will appear after the first animation. The imported clip might be longer than its animation. If so, split it after the animation and delete the unneeded portion. You can repeat these steps for the `move2` clip, placing it after the idle clip. In Figure 5.16, you can see that I have all of the clips in my file.

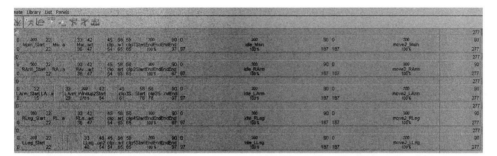

Figure 5.16 All three animations in a single file

Because I was careful to make sure that each clip started and stopped at the same pose, the blend between each clip is seamless. However, if yours is not quite as seamless as you would like, there is a Blend option.

1. Select two adjacent clips.

2. In the Trax Editor, go to **Create > Blend**.

As mentioned throughout this book, I cannot anticipate every specification that might occur in every project. However, in this chapter, I have shown you animation in its purest form, which (for the most part) will never change.

Maya in Games: Ratchet & Clank

Genre Action/Platform

Developer Insomniac

Publisher Sony

Platform PlayStation 2

The *Ratchet & Clank* series (*Ratchet & Clank*, *Ratchet & Clank 2*, and *Ratchet & Clank 3: Going Commando*) may look like your typical kid-friendly platform games. With its saturated color palette and cute characters, it recalls the traditions of classics like *Mario* or *Spyro the Dragon*. But after sitting down and playing the game, you'll notice quickly that *Ratchet & Clank* adds a heavy dose of shoot-'em-up action to the mix with dozens of weapons ranging from machine guns to rocket launchers to the "Rift Inducer," which actually creates mini-black holes that suck up enemies!

Because of its robust animation tools, Maya plays an important role in the game's action. Characters run and bop in an easy-to-read, cartoon fashion as bullets, missiles, and... well, black holes erupt around you. I highly recommend watching the character animation in this game as a key area of study.

Courtesy © 2004 Sony Computer Entertainment America Inc. "PlayStation" and the "PS" Family logo are registered trademarks of Sony Computer Entertainment Inc. and Ratchet & Clank®/© 2002 SCEAI. Developed by Insomniac Games.

The End?

Together we modeled a fearsome satyr warrior. We created textures of skin, leather, and metal. We fashioned a skeleton from joints and IK handles and animated him. We breathed life into what was once just pencil on paper. Is Silenus complete? Have we come to the end?

Not quite!

Particle Effects

Particle effects in games comprise the "visual cherry" that tops your artistic sundae. Correctly used, particle effects can suddenly bring visual flair and flash to what was once just a character running through a motion. Particle effects are used to add realistic details (such as dust, water spray, or even leaves blowing in the wind) that cannot be created with geometry.

Game particle effects are created using a number of different methods. However, most of them are created using particle editors developed by studios or packaged with commercial game engines.

For this project, use Maya's particles and geometry to mimic the kinds of particle effects that can be created with other applications.

Game Artist: Andrew Gerard

Job Title Artist

Studio Artifact Entertainment

Credits *Horizons: Empire of Istaria*

Studio Site http://www.artifact-entertainment.com/

Personal Site www.kinetifex.com

Q. How and why did you get into the game industry?

A. Since middle school, I knew I wanted to get into the game industry. I enjoy all aspects of games; the stories, artwork, music, sound, and of course, gameplay. I started messing around with editing games, and creating my own levels and artwork early on, primarily with the *Myth* and *Marathon* series. I really enjoyed making my own content for games. I went to school for an animation degree, landed a job, and now I make games professionally!

Q. Describe your role at your studio.

A. I'm an artist at Artifact Entertainment. I started out as the interface artist, creating icons and layout windows for *Horizons*. I was then moved over to the character team where I helped create characters and monsters by modeling, texturing, rigging, and animating. Currently, I'm doing everything art related for the game including modeling structures and other world objects.

Q. What has been the most inspirational to you in regard to your artwork?

A. I've always liked comic books and video games, and would have to say those are where I draw my artistic flavors from. I like the dark and gritty, semi-realistic art styles of games like *Quake 3*. The texture work in that game is just great. I enjoy Real-Time Strategy games with my favorite game series being the *Myth* series.

Q. What advice might you have for the up-and-coming game artist?

A. For an up-and-coming artist, I'd recommend having a strong foundation in the basics. Understand the anatomy for what you're going to be modeling. The way you put together models in 3D applications may change, but the structure and the way a human is put together doesn't. Also, get started making game content now. There are plenty of games out there with mod capabilities, as well as websites to get you started. The best way to learn how to make content for games is to do it.

Sprites

Sprites compose the vast majority of game particle effects. *Sprites* are like tiny planes that are textured to convey effects. In Maya, sprites always face the camera. This orientation makes them very useful for volumetric "cloudy" effects, such as smoke and dust.

Sprites, along with all other particles, are usually created using an emitter. *Emitters* are nonrendering objects that spit out particle streams. These streams can be adjusted in a variety of ways to control the particle emission direction, shape, speed, and other such attributes.

After particles are emitted, they can be affected by fields. *Fields* are dynamic forces that affect the physics of particles and other dynamic objects in a scene. Some examples are gravity, turbulence, and vortex (Figure 6.1).

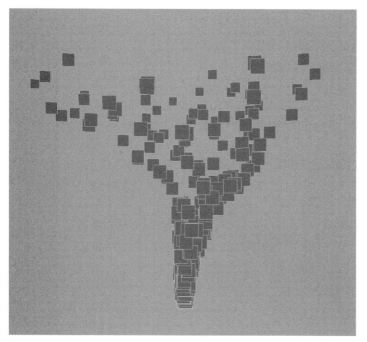

Figure 6.1 A sprite particle stream with a vortex field applied

Creating a Sprite Effect

The first effect you will create is the dust that Silenus kicks up when he moves his feet.

1.   ⊚   Open your finished animated model (or open the `10_Animations_Blended.mb` file in the `Tutorials\Chapter5\Character_Animation1\scenes\Steps` folder).

2. In the Dynamics module (F4), go to **Particles > Create Emitter**. Rename it **LFoot_Emitter**.

3. Point snap the emitter to the L_Hoof2 joint. Parent the emitter to the L_Hoof2 joint.

Before continuing, make sure your playback speed is set to Play Every Frame. You can find the playback options by going to **Window > Settings/Preferences > Preferences**. In the Preferences window, select the Timeline section in the left-hand list. Change the Playback Speed to Play Every Frame. With the playback speed set to Play Every Frame, the particles will emit properly as the animation plays. Playing the animation at the normal 30 frames-per-second (fps) with particles in the scene can cause the scene to skip, making the particle emission display incorrectly.

When you press Play, you'll notice that particles immediately begin spewing from the emitter attached to Silenus's left foot. You'll need to animate the emission so that the particles emit only when you want them to emit.

4. If you are using the provided file, go to frame 29. At this frame, Silenus takes a step back. With the LFoot_Emitter selected, change the Rate channel in the Channel Box to 800. Select the Rate channel, right-click it, and choose Key Selected from the menu that opens.

5. Go to frame 28. Change the Rate to 0, and set another key frame.

6. Go to frame 32, and enter 0 for the Rate, again setting a keyframe.

7. At frame 31, enter 400 for the Rate.

8. Change the Speed of the emitter to 3 and the Speed Random to 1.

Now, the emitter will emit a burst of particles for three frames when Silenus's foot takes a step back. The particles' speed of emission will be 3 units per second, plus or minus 1. By default, these particles are rendered as points. You'll need to change this to sprites.

9. Play the animation until some particles have emitted. Select the particles and open the Attribute Editor (Ctrl+A). Select the ParticleShape1 tab at the top of the Attribute Editor window if it's not active already.

10. Scroll down to the Render Attributes section and change Particle Render Type to Sprites. The points will become sprites in your scene (Figure 6.2). Click the Current Render Type button. New attributes will appear.

Figure 6.2 Sprite particles in the scene

Adjusting the Effect

Now that sprites are being emitted in the scene, you need to adjust their behavior and simulate a dust cloud.

1. At the moment, the particles emit in all directions, including down, below the ground on which Silenus is standing. With the emitter still selected, open the Attribute Editor.

2. Go to the Basic Emitter Attributes section under the Lfoot_Emitter tab. Change the Emitter Type to Directional. This causes the emitter to emit particles in a single direction rather than in all directions.

3. In the Distance/Direction Attributes section of the attributes, make the following changes:

    Direction X: 0.5

    Direction Y: 1.0

    Direction Z: -1.0

    Spread: 0.5

These attributes tell the emitter to direct its particles back and to Silenus's left side, which is the direction he steps. The Spread attribute has a minimum value of 0 and maximum value of 1. A spread of 0 means the particles will emit in a straight line. A spread of 1 means the particles will emit in a 180-degree area. Therefore, setting the spread to 0.5 will cause the particles to emit in a 90-degree arc.

Applying an Animated Sprite Texture

To create the appearance of dust, you can use a sequence of images that the sprite will use as its texture. This sequence will give the cloud of dust a more animated look.

1. Play the animation until some sprites are in the scene. Select the sprites. Name them **Dust_Sprite1**.

2. Go to **Particles > Sprite Wizard….**

   The Sprite Wizard will walk you through a series of steps to apply the animated texture to the selected sprites. Follow these steps:

   a. In the Image File Selection window, click the Browse button. Navigate to the CD and go to Images/Particles and choose the file named smoke.1.

   Because nine images in this folder have the same format (*filename.number*), Maya will automatically apply the Min and Max settings of 1 and 9, respectively, indicating an animated image sequence.

   Click Continue.

> **Note:** Make sure you name the sprite texture sequences using the *filename.number* convention (for example, fire.8). The image formats need to be either TIFF or Targa so that the alpha channel will be available to render as a transparency map. The extensions (.tif or .tga) should not be in the filename unless they are followed by the number of the sequence (for example, fire.tga.8).

   b. In the Image Assignment window, choose Cycle Through the Images for Each Particle if it is not selected already.

   This tells Maya to animate the sequence of images on each sprite.

   Click Continue.

   c. In the Initial Sprite Assignment window, choose Use the First Image in the Sequence from the available options.

   The image sequence for the dust is rendered in a particular order so that the visual effect will look right. Other options allow you to choose a random start from any of the sequence of images for each sprite.

   Click Continue.

d. The Animation Assignment window offers a number of options for how the particles will *interpolate* (how the animation will calculate) between each other. Choose Ease-In/Ease-Out Increasing.

The different interpolation options can have very different looks. At some point, you may want to experiment to see what works best under what circumstances. Using Ease-In/Ease-Out Increasing will smooth the transition between images in the sequence as the sequence increases.

Also, make certain Cycle Only Once During Lifespan is selected.

Click Continue.

e. The last window gives you a Summary of your options. Review them. If you approve, click Apply.

Make sure Smooth Shading (**5** key) and Hardware Texturing (**6** key) are on so you can see the smoke images on the sprites. You now have an animated sequence of smoke applied to the sprites (Figure 6.3).

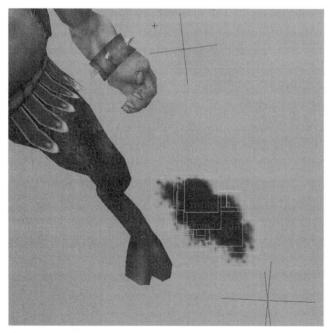

Figure 6.3 The sprites with an image sequence applied

Adjusting the Particle's Appearance

Let's adjust the overall look of the particles, beginning with their color and how long they last.

1. Select the sprites, and open the Attribute Editor. Choose the Dust_SpriteShape1 tab. These attributes contain most of the behavior options for the particles.

2. Go to the Lifespan Attributes section. You may notice that the Lifespan Mode option is being controlled and can't be edited. This is because the Sprite Wizard was used to apply the texture sequence. Right-click on the *name* Lifespan Mode (not the attribute's value) in the Channel Box, and choose Break Connections from the menu that opens. This returns control of the attribute to you.

3. Make the following adjustments:

    Lifespan Mode: Random range

    Lifespan: 1

    Lifespan Random: 0.25

    These options make the sprites live for 1 second, plus or minus a quarter of a second.

    If you play the animation now, the sprites should not disappear simultaneously.

4. Go to the Add Dynamic Attributes section. Click the Opacity button. In the Particle Opacity window that opens, check the Add Per Particle Attribute option, and click the Add Attribute button.

5. In the Per Particle (Array) Attributes section, a new option called opacityPP appears. In the text box next to opacityPP, right-click and choose Create Ramp from the window that opens.

    If you play the animation now, you'll see that rather than just disappearing, the particles actually fade away as their lifespan comes to an end. This effect (applying a Ramp texture to their opacity) makes them look more natural. A *ramp* blends between two or more colors, by default blending between black and white.

Note: Many different options appear in the Per Particle (Array) Attributes section of the particle's Attribute Editor. You can also create quite a few more. Dozens of particle options, commands, and controls can be created; however, we will go over only the ones that are important to our project. Feel free to experiment with the different options available.

Changing the Sprite Color

Now that the sprites look like smoke, let's change their color to look more like dust or dirt.

1. Back in the Add Dynamic Attributes section of the particle's Attribute Editor, click the Color button. In the Particle Color window that opens, check the Add Per Particle Attribute option and click Add Attribute. The rgbPP option appears in the Per Particle (Array) Attributes section.

2. As you did with opacityPP, right-click in the text box next to rgbPP and choose Create Ramp.

   By default, this ramp creates a blend between red, green, and blue. They are not the best colors to use for dirt or dust, so you'll need to adjust the ramp colors.

3. Right-click on the text box next to rgbPP, and choose **<-arrayMapper2.out-ColorPP > Edit Ramp** from the window that opens. The ramp attributes open in the Attribute Editor (Figure 6.4).

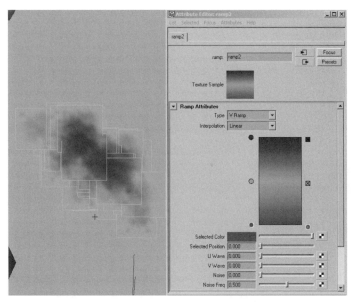

Figure 6.4 The default rgbPP ramp settings

Using ramps to control different attributes of particles such as opacity and color can be much easier than using manual control and keyframing. The top of the ramp represents the end of the particle's lifespan (or "death") while the bottom represents the beginning (or "birth").

You should see three markers in the ramp, one each at the top, middle, and bottom. Selecting the circles on the left side of the ramp will let you move their positions, changing the blending order. Clicking on the box on the right side of the ramp will delete the marker.

To change their color, select each marker, and adjust the Selected Color attribute below the ramp. You can delete the middle marker, and make the top marker a light brown color and the bottom marker a darker brown. However, the color of the original textures is very black. You'll need to adjust it for the color to show through.

1. Select the sprites. In the Attribute Editor, use the arrow tabs at the top of the window to scroll to the right. Open the File96 tab. It may be named differently for you.

2. Under the Color Balance section, raise the Color Offset attribute from black to a lighter gray.

When you play the animation now, the ramp colors should show up much better (Figure 6.5). When the sprites are born, they are a dark brown color. They fade to a lighter color as they die.

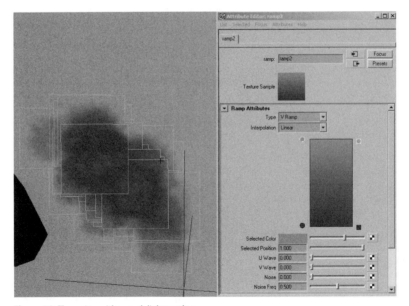

Figure 6.5 The sprites with a much lighter color

Animating the Sprite Size

You can also use a ramp to animate the size of the sprites.

1. Back in the Add Dynamic Attributes section of the sprites' Attribute Editor, click the General button.

2. In the Add Attribute window that opens, choose the Particle tab at the top. You can see the many different attributes available for particles. From the list, choose spriteScaleXPP and spriteScaleYPP. Click OK. As before, these new options appear in the Per Particle (Array) Attributes section.

3. In each, right-click the corresponding text boxes and choose Create Ramp from the menu that opens.

If you play the animation now, the sprites are large at birth, and shrink as they die. You actually want them to do the opposite to simulate a real dust cloud.

4. Right-click on the text box next to the spriteScaleYPP, and follow the menu to Edit Ramp.

5. The ramp shows a black-to-white gradient with three markers. Delete the middle marker by clicking on the box on the right side of the ramp. Using the circular marker handles on the left side of the ramp, move the colors to opposite positions, making the color blend white-to-black instead.

6. Select the white color's marker, and click on the white box next to Selected Color. In the Color Chooser window that opens, you can see the H, S, and V text boxes. These indicate Hue, Saturation, and Value. Increase the Value from 1 to 2. This makes the value of white being used twice the normal range and will double the size of the sprites as they die.

> **Note:** Most sliders in Maya have minimum and maximum thresholds that can be overridden by manual control. If you find a slider only goes so far, feel free to manually type in a higher or lower value. You'll find that it works in most cases.

7. Select the black color's marker, and click on the black box next to Select Color. Change the Value from 0 to 0.5. This way, the sprites will be born a little larger than before.

8. Repeat Steps 1 through 7 for the spriteScaleXPP attribute.

If you play the animation now, you should find that the sprites grow as they fade away, adding to the cloudy look (Figure 6.6).

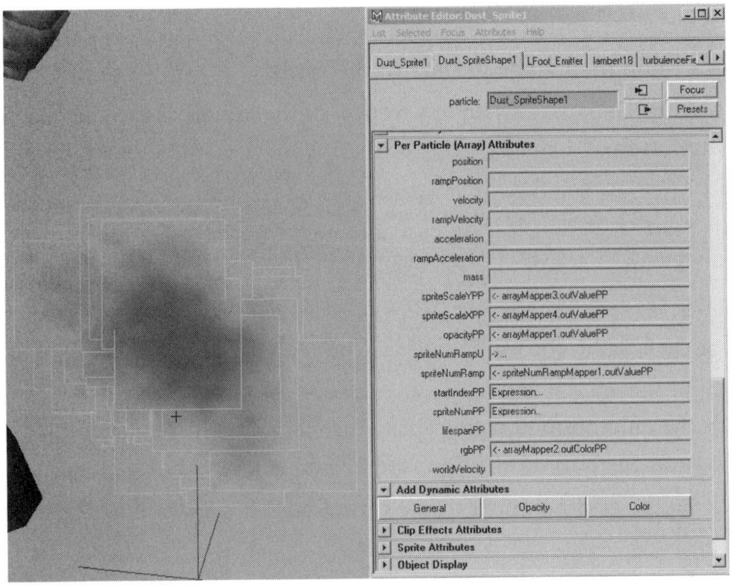

Figure 6.6 The sprites increase in size as they fade away.

Applying Fields

As mentioned earlier, fields are dynamic forces (such as gravity and turbulence) that are applied to particles and other dynamic objects. In this dust cloud example, you can use gravity and turbulence to simulate realistic effects.

1. Select the Dust_Sprite1 particles, and go to **Fields > Turbulence**. This creates a Turbulence field in your scene. You may want to move it out from under the character so you can have better access to it during the animation.

2. With the turbulence field selected, change the Magnitude channel to 20 in the Channel Box. This increases the effect of the field. Even so, the effect of turbulence is fairly subtle.

3. Select the particles again, and go to **Fields > Gravity**. This creates a gravity field in your scene. Again, you may want to move it away from the character for easy access.

Note: By default, a gravity field's magnitude is set to 9.8, which simulates gravity on earth for most solid objects. If the gravity field (or any other field) doesn't seem to affect your particles, then they are most likely being cached into memory. In order for fields to affect particles, choose **Solvers > Memory Caching > Delete** before applying the fields.

Play the animation. The dust particles fall immediately after being emitted. Because dust clouds are significantly lighter than solid objects, you can lower the gravity field's magnitude to indicate this.

4. Change the gravity field's magnitude channel to 2.5. Now the dust cloud falls much more gradually.

You've finished your first particle effect. The procedure for creating such an effect can be awkward at first, but should come easier with practice. Let's make a second dust effect for when Silenus steps forward.

Creating a Second Effect

The emitter is already in place, and the sprites are set up to create another dust effect for when Silenus steps forward. Creating another dust cloud can be just a matter of animating the emitter's rate and direction.

1. Go to frame 53. Key the Rate of the LFoot_Emitter with a value of 0.

2. At frame 54, change the Rate to 100, setting a keyframe.

3. At frame 59, set the Rate to 50, setting a keyframe.

4. At frame 60, set the Rate to 0, setting another keyframe.

If you play the animation now, a second burst of particles will emit when Silenus steps forward. However, it's still emitting backward, and to the left. You'll need to animate the emitter's direction to change this.

5. Back at frame 32, open the Attribute Editor for the emitter. In the Distance/Direction Attributes section, right-click on the Direction X, Direction Y, Direction Z, and Spread attributes of the emitter. Choose Set Key from the menu that opens.

6. Do so again at frame 53.

7. At frame 54, make the following changes, setting keys as you go:

Direction X: 0.5

Direction Y: 1

Direction Z: 0.5

Spread: 1

You now have a second, smaller dust cloud for when Silenus steps forward.

Continuing the Dust Effect

Go ahead and continue the dust effect for the rest of the animation. Repeat the previous steps, keyframing the Rate of the LFoot_Emitter as Silenus runs forward. You also need to add a second emitter for the right foot. The setup for the right foot is the same as for the left, but you do not need to create a second particle system for the other foot.

1. Repeat the steps in the "Creating a Sprite Effect" section, creating a new emitter, but parenting it to the R_Hoof2 joint and naming it **RFoot_Emitter** instead.

2. Play the animation for a few frames, select the new particles that emit from the R_Foot_Emitter, and delete them.

3. Go to **Window > Relationship Editors > Dynamic Relationships…**. In the Dynamic Relationships window that opens, select the Dust_Sprite1 particle from the list on the left side.

4. In the right pane, click the Emitters selection mode, and select the RFoot_Emitter.

This makes the Dust_Sprite1 particle emit from *both* emitters. Now you just need to animate the RFoot_Emitter's rate and direction as you did with the LFoot_Emitter. Set them to emit in time with the steps Silenus takes to make his second sword attack.

The particles probably won't look exactly right when the character is walking in place. Remember the character will actually be walking forward in the game engine, and the particles will trail correctly.

Game Artist: Andrew Risch

Job Title Architectural Artist

Studio Sony Online Entertainment

Credits *PlanetSide, PlanetSide: Core Combat, Star Wars Galaxies: Jump to Lightspeed*

Studio Site www.sonyonline.com

Personal Site www.polycount.com

Q. How and why did you get into the game industry?

A. The how: I got into the industry after running my website for several years. At the time, I was a traditional architect doing the typical hotels, office buildings, and occasional school or fancy house. I had made numerous friends and contacts throughout the industry through the community around polycount.com. Eventually someone at Sony decided that I might be valuable at doing virtual buildings and offered me a job.

The why: I wanted to do it because I was in love with video games. My affair begins stereotypically with an adventure with *Pong* in the late 1970s, and I was hooked. I had been messing around with editing games on the side for a while as a serious hobby at the time. I had decided that if I didn't give it a shot when/if I had a chance that it would be something I would regret.

Continues

Game Artist: Andrew Risch *(continued)*

Q. Describe your role at your studio.

A. I design and build environmental assets, specializing in architecture.

Q. What has been the most inspirational to you in regard to your artwork?

A. I draw my inspiration from the designers I work with. I treat them as my clients. They have a need, be it atmosphere, gameplay, some sort of goal in mind. I try to understand and absorb their needs and then design that into the buildings and environments I am responsible for. It is not as simple as "form follows function," but that is the easiest way to put it.

Q. What is your favorite artistic style?

A. Anything bold and larger than life. I believe that if you are going to go through the effort, say it as large as you can.

Q. What is your favorite kind of game?

A. Massively Multi-Player Online Games (MMOG's) and shooters. I love the large worlds of a MMOG. The sheer volume and epic size compared to a "normal" game keeps me up late at night. Shooters for the quick adrenaline fix. Although I am also a sucker for any *Zelda* or *Mario* game; they are like pure gameplay between the sheets.

Q. How do you use Maya in your specific job?

A. All our exporting and shader tools were built into Maya. It becomes the platform on which assets are built, set up technically, and exported into our databases for the world builders to access.

Q. What about Maya do you like better than other 3D apps?

A. The one feature of Maya that stands out for me is the ability to make simple scripts to help me with my day-to-day efforts. Cut and paste it from the listener and it works. Throw it up on a shelf and even make a custom button within minutes. It helps me make the tool a bit of my own easily.

Q. Which Maya tool could you not live without?

A. I have a love/hate relationship with the hard and soft edges tools in Maya. They can be a real pain and take a lot of effort to do on more irregular geometry. However, once they are set up properly, it is quite attractive.

Q. What advice might you have for the up-and-coming game artist?

A. When looking for a job, please remember that the games that you are trying to get a job on today will not be coming out for at least a year if not more. Aim your portfolio's content at the type and sophistication of art assets that will be typical in a year. Employers want to hire people that can make that sort of art today.

Geometry Effects

Another method of creating effects in a game is to use textured geometry where sprites alone won't work. For example, you can create a "swish" effect to add a bit of flash to the sword's attack swings.

1. Create a polygon plane, and rename it to **Swish**. Apply a new Lambert material to it, and rename it Swish_Texture.

2. ⬯ Map the material's color attribute with the swish_1.tga file from the Images/Particles folder on the CD.

3. Go to frame 33, when Silenus's first sword swing is at its farthest. Scale and rotate the plane to fit the swish image with the sword's position, as in Figure 6.7.

4. Keyframe the Translate, Rotate, and Scale channels of the plane at their set position. Your settings may vary.

    TranslateX: 0

    TranslateY: 7.1

    TranslateZ: -2.1

    RotateX: 57

    RotateY: 110.7

    RotateZ: -4.2

    ScaleX, Y, and Z: 24

5. Keyframe the Alpha Gain attribute of the swish texture under the Color Balance section in the Attributes.

6. At frame 25, rotate and scale the plane as follows (again, your settings may vary):

    TranslateX: -1.85

    TranslateY: 5.65

    TranslateZ: -1.15

    RotateX: 162.7

    RotateY: 173

    RotateZ: 118.4

    ScaleX, Y, and Z: 13.2

Figure 6.7 The swish plane positioned on the character

7. Set the swish texture's Alpha Gain to 0, and set a keyframe.

8. At frame 40, rotate the plane a little further in the Y direction, scaling the plane larger to about 31 in all three scale directions. Key the Alpha Gain back down to 0.

Now, you can see that the plane rotates and scales larger with the swing of the sword. It also fades into and out of view as the swing finishes. You can repeat these steps for the other swings, orienting the plane to correspond with each attack and animating the Alpha Gain of the texture to control the transparency.

Creating Impact Effects

You can use geometry for other types of visual effects. You can create impact effects for Silenus's sword, as if he were striking an enemy.

1. Create a polygonal cylinder. Delete all of the faces except one of the caps.

2. Planar map the cap from the Y direction, and apply a new Lambert material. Name it **Impact_Texture**. Name the object **Impact**.

3.    Map the material's color attribute with the `flair_1.tga` file found in the `Images/Particles` folder on the CD.

4.   Push the cap's center vertex down, creating a cone shape. Go to frame 28. Position the Impact object as shown in Figure 6.8.

Figure 6.8 The impact object positioned in the scene

At this point, you need to key the Alpha Gain of the texture to control transparency and animate the object's position, similarly to what you did with the swish object.

5.   At its current position, key the Translate channels of the Impact object. Also, key the Alpha Gain of the texture at a value of 1.

6.   At frames 25 and 31, key the Alpha Gain to 0.

7.   At frame 25, scale the Impact object to 2, setting a keyframe. At frame 31, increase the scale to 5, setting another keyframe.

This has created a flashing impact effect that fades into and out of view, increasing in size. Repeat these steps for the other swings as you see fit—animating the transparency, position, and scale each time.

In a real game situation, you would create effects like the dust cloud, sword swish, and impact effects one time, and the game would then replay the effect each time it was triggered during gameplay.

Additional Helpful CD Files

The companion CD includes many extra files that you can use for further practice as you increase your game art skills. For example, under `Images/Particles`, you'll find more sprite texture examples.

Under `Video/Animation_Reference`, you'll find three more video sequences of my friend Arvee running through sword attack moves. You can use these files when you practice making more animations.

Finally, in the Images folder, you'll find great high-resolution photos that you can use as modeling references or texture sources.

Final Thoughts

Well, you've come to the end of the road. You've taken a concept on a piece of paper and made it into a living, moving creature that can be used in a video game. I recommend that all aspiring game artists add this kind of project to their portfolios. It runs through the entire gamut of the game art pipeline:

- Concept to Modeling
- Modeling to Texturing
- Texturing to Rigging
- Rigging to Animation
- Animation to Effects

Now all you need is a programmer to come along and plug Silenus into a game!

When you build your own portfolio, focus on one or two aspects of the pipeline that are your specialty (modeling and texturing for example). However, make sure you have a good working knowledge of the entire pipeline. You never know when you will be called upon to work on something that is out of your normal jurisdiction. The more easily you can make that leap, the better your standing in your studio's art department will be.

I encourage you to work on a variety of game art subjects: buildings, vehicles, weapons, etc. Don't just focus on characters. While they're fun to make, they really are just one part of the art requirements that all games have.

I hope you've enjoyed creating Silenus the Satyr Warrior, and I hope you learned a lot about how the game art production pipeline works.

Maya in Games: Jak 3

Genre Adventure Platformer

Developer Naughty Dog

Publisher Sony

Platform Playstation 2

The *Jak & Daxter* series of games (*Jak & Daxter: The Precursor Legacy*, *Jak 2*, and *Jak 3*) have been widely touted as some of the more innovative platform games to have come out in recent years. It includes atypical elements such as hovercraft racing, turret gunning, and car jacking. Starring Jak and his wise-cracking sidekick Daxter, you play through sprawling, beautiful platform environments, fighting enemies along the way.

Aside from the fantastic animation, the environments are really what I would recommend studying in this game. The sheer amount of detail that each model and texture has is very impressive, and that you can see for great distances makes it even more eye-catching.

Index

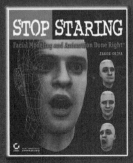

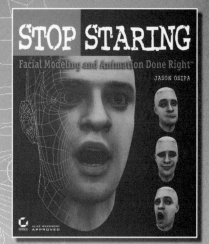
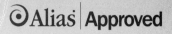